THE
HOUR MAGAZINE
COOKBOOK

THE
HOUR MAGAZINE
COOKBOOK

Gary Collins

EDITOR: Catherine R. Pomponio

EXECUTIVE EDITOR: Martin M. Berman

G. P. PUTNAM'S SONS
New York

G. P. Putnam's Sons
200 Madison Avenue
New York, NY 10016

Photographs by Michael Leshnov

Library of Congress Cataloging in Publication Data

Collins, Gary, date.
The Hour magazine cookbook.

Includes index.
1. Cookery.   I. Hour magazine (Television
program)   II. Title
TX715.C7215   1985   641.5   85-16692
ISBN 0-399-13083-7

Printed in the United States of America

1   2   3   4   5   6   7   8   9   10

Acknowledgments

Since this recipe book exists only because there was *first* a television show, it has taken a cooperative effort from both the people involved with putting this book together and those who were originally involved with putting the cooking segments together for the show. They all must be thanked. I'm grateful to the entire staff at *Hour Magazine*—for their contributions over the years, for their perseverance in finding outstanding guests to perform in the cooking segments and for their commitment to making each segment a worthwhile one.

I'd like to give special thanks to the following people:

• to Yvonne Collier Alvarez for her painstaking efforts in tracking down recipes of the guests who participated, and for her enthusiasm about this project;

• to Debbie Hoy and Beth Dong, who helped with the cookbook from its inception;

• to the segment producers, whose efforts over the years managed to keep the cooking spots fresh and exciting—Karen Cadle, Larry Ferber, Margie Friedman, Sue Solomon and Bob Carman;

• to Paul Nichols and his promotion staff for all their help in putting this book together;

• to the over 1 million viewers who have requested recipes over the years and have actually asked for this book;

• and finally, to Ed Vane for his overall support and continuing guidance.

*To Chris Circosta—without his expertise
and professionalism this collection of
recipes could not have happened.*

Contents

2. CELEBRITIES 97

Introduction

When *Hour Magazine* went on the air in September of 1980, we were filled with both excitement and anxiety. We were excited by the challenge of producing a new kind of daytime talk show that would offer viewers practical information in an entertaining manner. But we were anxious because most of the long-running talk shows seemed to be losing their audiences. In 1980 we saw no fewer than forty-nine new shows coming out of the starting gate. Five years later, I'm proud to say that *Hour Magazine* is the only show of those forty-nine still on the air!

While there are many reasons for our success, the most consistent audience pleaser offered by *Hour Magazine* has been our cooking segments. During the first few months of the program, we offered the recipes prepared on the show. Within a month, our offices were literally swamped with over 250,000 requests.

We tried many ways of responding to this overwhelming demand. First we enlisted the help of handicapped workers in our area. Then we tried bringing in an army of high school and college students on weekends to attack the problem. But both efforts were unsuccessful. Finally we hit upon a great idea: We decided to publish a month's worth of recipes in one booklet. We have processed well over a million requests to date.

For years we've been asked, Why don't you put all the recipes in one volume? At last, we've done just that! While we couldn't include all of the recipes presented on *Hour Magazine*, we have selected some of our favorites. In compiling them, we noticed a trend toward health-consciousness. So you'll find less salt, less beef, more poultry and seafood; less frying and more broiling and grilling. The recipes seem to reflect the population's preoccupation with healthful and nutritious meals.

I also thought this would be an appropriate time to clear up some of the questions I'm asked most frequently, no matter where I travel. These three come up continually:

1. Your response is always positive—do you *really* like everything that's made?
2. How do you stay so thin when you're always tasting everything?
3. Did Chicken Dog really taste that bad?

My answers to numbers 1 and 2 can be combined. Remember that everything is freshly prepared for the taping of the show. Remember that, though everything made may not be of gourmet caliber, my guests usually bring a recipe that's been successful in their kitchens or their restaurants. And, most important, remember that I do take just one or two bites of everything—I hate to spoil my appetite and I usually head home right after the taping of the show to have dinner with my family. So you can understand my appreciative reactions—and my ability to stay thin despite the weekly tastings. Finally for the answer to question number 3—you'll have to wait until you get to page 142 and judge for yourself. In the meantime, enjoy the recipes that follow. If they provide you, your family and guests with some nutritious and pleasurable meals, then our efforts will have been worthwhile! And don't forget . . . make every meal count!

Gary Collins

THE
HOUR MAGAZINE
COOKBOOK

1

CHEFS, GASTRONOMES AND RESTAURATEURS

As you'll see from the following pages, most of the guests whom we invite into *Hour*'s kitchen are chefs or restaurateurs or cookbook authors. I can always be assured that the dishes they prepare will be extraordinary, and I'll get to taste a "house" specialty or see a favorite recipe of a great chef evolve.

We've chosen an interesting mix for you to try—from Poor Man's Caviar to classics like Lemon Chicken and Eggplant Parmesan. But each recipe brings with it the style and special ingredients of its presenter. I think you'll enjoy them.

SHE was the singer whose hit song "Teach Me Tonight" rose to number one on the charts. And she performed with the late Spike Jones. Now **Helen Grayco** and her husband, Bill Rosen, own a very successful restaurant here in Los Angeles, called GATSBY'S. She brought us the recipe for their famous Cheese Toast Gatsby—sure to whet your appetite for any meal that follows.

Cheese Toast Gatsby

1 stick (½ cup) butter, melted
4 cloves garlic, finely diced
½ teaspoon ground chili pepper
1 cup grated cheese (combination of Cheddar/Swiss/
    Romano)
1 loaf French bread, sliced diagonally

Preheat broiler. Combine butter, garlic and chili pepper in saucepan over low heat. Brush onto bread. Sprinkle cheese on bread and place on baking sheet. Place in oven under broiler for 5 minutes, or until cheese is melted. Serve immediately.

Serves 12–14.

HELEN GRAYCO

SMOKED Ham Mousse sounds a bit complicated to prepare, but the taste is worth it. Culinary authority **Michele Braden** made it when she visited *Hour Magazine;* she told me that it can be prepared several days in advance and refrigerated. It's served as an appetizer, along with thinly sliced cucumbers, assorted mustards, watercress, sliced breads, melbas or crackers. Sounds good, doesn't it?

Smoked Ham Mousse

1½ envelopes unflavored gelatin
¼ cup Paul Masson Madeira
2 tablespoons butter
2–4 tablespoons shallots, minced
2 cloves garlic, minced
2 or 3 chicken livers, cleaned and soaked in milk or wine for at least 1 hour
11 ounces smoked ham, trimmed, cut in 1-inch pieces
¼ cup butter
1½ tablespoons Dijon mustard, or to taste
1¾ cups heavy cream
¼ teaspoon thyme
½ teaspoon dill weed
Salt and pepper to taste
Grated rind of 2 lemons
¼ cup Japanese dried mushrooms, rehydrated and thinly sliced

Pour gelatin over the Madeira and let soften. In a skillet, melt 2 tablespoons butter and sauté shallots and garlic until soft. Add livers and sauté until just pink on the inside. In food processor fitted with metal blade, process livers, ham, ¼ cup butter and mustard until smooth. Add gelatin and blend. Add cream and process until blended. Add remaining ingredients and process briefly so as not to destroy the texture of lemon rind or mushrooms. Pour into oiled mold or molds and chill until set, about 6 hours.

Makes about 3 cups.

MICHELE BRADEN

Lox Mousse

2 ounces lox
¼ cup black olives, pitted and sliced
2 tablespoons minced onion
1 pound cream cheese, whipped
2 teaspoons lemon juice
Freshly ground pepper

Reserve a piece of the lox and a few olives for garnish (see below). In a food processor, blend together lox, onion and cream cheese. Add lemon juice and pepper. Blend briefly. Fold olives into above mixture. Garnish mousse with reserved piece of lox and sliced black olives.

Note

Lox is also known as smoked salmon.

Makes about 2 cups.

SUSAN MENDELSON

THE owner of MISCHA'S RUSSIAN RESTAURANT, **Michael "Mischa" Markarian,** brought us his version of Poor Man's Caviar. I challenge you to try this one at a dinner party, and I'll bet the comments you hear will all be positive ones!

Poor Man's Caviar (Baklajanaya Ikra)

2 medium eggplants
2 medium tomatoes
2 medium bell peppers
1 small onion, chopped
1 clove garlic, minced
2 tablespoons tomato paste
Salt and pepper to taste
Parsley
Cherry tomatoes
Greek olives
Lemon wedges

Puncture eggplants on all sides. Bake for 45 minutes at 375°. Bake tomatoes and bell peppers for 20 minutes at 375°.

Brown onion and garlic. Peel eggplants and tomatoes. Peel bell peppers, then remove seeds and core. Coarse grind eggplants, tomatoes, bell peppers, cooked onion and garlic. Add tomato paste and salt and pepper. Combine and cook over low flame for about 5 minutes, stirring occasionally. Cool and garnish with parsley, cherry tomatoes, Greek olives and lemon wedges.

Serves 10.

MISCHA MARKARIAN

DANCING, singing and cooking—you can find plenty of all three at a popular Greek restaurant in Los Angeles, called THE GALLEON. The owner, **Dean Katsenes,** visited *Hour's* kitchen and demonstrated the elements of a Greek good time. He presented Spanakopitas—an hors d'oeuvre à la grecque.

Spanakopitas

1 onion, finely chopped
2 sticks (1 cup) butter, melted
3 8-ounce packages frozen chopped spinach
¼ cup minced parsley
¼ teaspoon dill (optional)
8 ounces cottage cheese
¾ pound feta cheese, crumbled
3 eggs
½ pound filo pastry leaves

Preheat over to 375°. Cook onion in ¼ cup butter until transparent. Combine spinach, parsley, dill, cheeses, eggs and onion, and mix well with your hands. Take a filo leaf, brush lightly with melted butter and fold into thirds. Lightly butter top surface. Place 1 tablespoon of cheese-spinach mixture at bottom of strip and fold corner up to form triangle. Continue folding in triangle shape until strip is completely folded. Repeat process until all ingredients are used. Place triangles on baking sheet. Brush each lightly with melted butter. Bake for 15–20 minutes, or until golden brown.

Makes 50 pieces.

DEAN KATSENES

Grape Leaves

100 grape leaves
  1 cup uncooked rice
1½ pounds lamb (not too lean), coarsely ground
  1 tablespoon salt
    Pepper, cinnamon, allspice to taste
  2 lemons

Wash grape leaves and pour boiling water over the leaves to soften them. Wash and drain rice. Mix together rice, lamb, salt, spices and juice of 1 lemon. Place about 1 tablespoon of rice-meat mixture on the veined side of each grape leaf. Spread across in a line, turn in the sides of the leaf and roll up completely. Line bottom of pan with 3 or 4 grape leaves on a pan rack. Place rolls evenly in rows, arranging in layers, each layer crisscrossing the last. Use an inverted plate to hold down rolls. Add water to cover. Bring to boil; then reduce heat to low and cook stuffed leaves 20–30 minutes. Add juice of remaining lemon 5 minutes before removing from heat. Can be served with a side dish of leban (yogurt).

Makes about 100.

LARRY NICOLA

Quizza (Quiche and Pizza)

1½ ⅗-ounce cakes fresh compressed yeast
  1 cup lukewarm water

4 cups all-purpose flour
1 teaspoon salt
¼ cup vegetable oil

In a bowl, dissolve yeast in water. Add just enough flour to make a soft, smooth batter. Cover bowl. Leave in a warm place so the batter can rise—about 30 minutes. Sift together remaining flour and salt, and make a well in the middle of it. Fill with risen batter and oil, and mix thoroughly. Knead vigorously, adding a little more water if necessary, until dough is smooth and elastic. Roll into a ball and place in a large bowl. Leave covered with a damp cloth in a warm place for 2 hours, or until dough has doubled in bulk.

Lightly flatten risen dough. Roll out about 12–14 ounces of dough evenly with the fingers until it stretches to cover sides as well as bottom of a well-oiled 9-inch by 1-inch deep French quiche pan, as for a deep-dish pie. The edges should extend slightly over pan edge to create a crown when filled. Place on baking sheet and chill.

Quiche Filling

4 ounces Gruyère cheese, coarsely grated or thinly sliced
4 ounces Swiss cheese, coarsely grated or thinly sliced
3 eggs
1 cup milk, scalded
1 cup heavy cream
2 tablespoons all-purpose flour
½ teaspoon salt
Dash white pepper
¼ teaspoon nutmeg

Preheat oven to 375°. Line bottom of dough shell with cheeses. In a bowl, mix eggs, milk, cream, flour, salt, pepper and nutmeg. Beat well. Pour mixture over cheese. Bake in oven for about 30 minutes, or until custard is set and golden brown on top.

Serves 4–6.

JOE ITALIANO

PIZZA has always been a favorite of mine. **Chef Keith Divino,** of MICELI'S ITALIAN RESTAURANT & PIZZERIA in Hollywood, showed us how to make one, from the twirling to the enjoying!

Pizza Divino

Dough

> 1 package dry yeast
> 1 cup lukewarm water
> 1 teaspoon granulated sugar
> 1 teaspoon salt
> 1½ cups all-purpose flour, approximately

Sauce

> 2 cups pizza sauce (unseasoned or basil only), *or* 1 cup tomato puree and 1 cup ground whole tomatoes
> 3 teaspoons salt
> 2 teaspoons black pepper
> 1 teaspoon garlic powder
> 1 teaspoon oregano
> 2 teaspoons granulated sugar
> 2 teaspoons grated Parmesan cheese
> 3 teaspoons olive oil

Toppings

> ¾ cup shredded mozzarella cheese, or to taste
> Pepperoni, sausage, etc., to taste

In a mixing bowl, sprinkle yeast over warm water and let stand 5 minutes to soften. Add sugar and salt, and beat well. Add 1½ cups flour and beat until smooth. Add just enough more flour to make a dough just barely firm enough to handle. Knead until smooth. Divide the dough into thirds. Knead each piece into a ball. Let rise 30 minutes.

Preheat oven to 425°. In a small bowl, mix together all sauce ingredients. Flatten one ball of dough, then pull and stretch gently to fit a lightly greased 9-inch layer-cake tin. Press edges of dough to make a slight rim. Brush on a thin layer of sauce (to taste). Cover with mozzarella cheese and add any other toppings desired, such as pepperoni, sausage, etc. *Suggestion:* Canadian bacon and pineapple.

Repeat process with remaining balls of dough. Bake for about 25 minutes.

Makes 3 9-inch pizzas.

CHEF KEITH HULL DIVINO

ONE of my guests went from 320 pounds to 150 pounds, and he wrote a diet book called *Controlled Cheating: The Fats Goldberg Take It Off, Keep It Off Diet Program.* **Larry Goldberg,** who's known as New York's Pizza King, brought a little bit of New York to *Hour Magazine* when he prepared this pizza fit for "royalty"!

King and Queen Royal Crown Pizza

Dough

    4 level scoops Ragú Pizza Quick Crust Mix
⅓ cup very warm water
    Vegetable oil

Topping

    4 tablespoons Ragú Chunky Style Pizza Quick Sauce, Big Combo
    2 slices (about 2 ounces) American cheese, cut in half
    4 tablespoons Ragú Chunky Style Pizza Quick Sauce, The Works
    4 slices (about 2 ounces) sharp Cheddar cheese

Prepare crust mix according to label directions, using 4 level scoops mix and ⅓ cup very warm water. Preheat toaster oven to 375° while dough rises. Divide dough into 4 equal pieces. Press dough evenly into 4 oiled 4-inch tart pans, forming scalloped edges. To assemble each crown, spoon 1 tablespoon Pizza Quick Sauce, Big Combo, onto each pizza crust. Top with ½ slice American cheese. Evenly spread 1 tablespoon Pizza Quick Sauce, The

Works, over cheese. Top with 1 slice Cheddar cheese. Bake directly on oven rack for 25 minutes, or until bottom of crust is golden.

Makes 4 pizza crowns.

LARRY GOLDBERG

Printed by permission of Ragú & Goldberg Pizzerias © 1985.

A few years ago, a treat that originated in France arrived in America. And now croissants are everywhere—in supermarkets, bakeries, and specialty shops springing up all over the country. **John Francis,** the Director of Consumer Information for the National Livestock and Meat Board, visited and told us how to make a "proper" croissant sandwich. He proved that croissants aren't just for breakfast.

West Coast Croissant Sandwich

½ small ripe avocado, seeded and peeled
1 tablespoon prepared creamy cucumber dressing
6 thin slices Canadian-style bacon
2 large spinach leaves
2 thin slices red onion
1 whole-wheat croissant, split lengthwise

Mash avocado in small bowl. Stir in cucumber dressing. To assemble sandwich, layer 3 slices Canadian-style bacon, spinach leaves, red onion and remaining bacon over bottom half of croissant. Spoon avocado mixture on top. Close sandwich with top of croissant.

Serves 1.

PRESENTED BY JOHN FRANCIS

Printed by permission of National Livestock & Meat Board. Copyright © 1984 by National Livestock & Meat Board.

A few years ago, we invited champion garlic cook **Jo Stallard** to our studios to prepare her prize-winning garlic soup. She had just won the Gilroy Garlic Festival, and I wanted to try my hand at making soup, using her recipe. The soup is unusual and a garlic-lover's delight. And I think we even proved the old idea that garlic *does* have medicinal powers. For weeks after Jo's presentation, no one on the staff got sick!

Jo's Baked Garlic Soup

      2 cups diced tomatoes
    3–5 zucchini, sliced
      ½ green pepper, diced
      ½ teaspoon paprika
      1 teaspoon basil
    4–5 cloves garlic, minced
      1 can (approximately 15 ounces) garbanzo beans, undrained
      2 onions, sliced
    1½ cups dry white wine
      2 teaspoons salt
    1–2 bay leaves
      1 cup grated Romano cheese
    1¼ cups grated Monterey Jack cheese
    1¼ cups heavy cream

Preheat oven to 375°. Butter a 3-quart (or larger) baking dish. Mix all ingredients, except the cheeses and cream, in dish. Cover and bake for 1 hour.

Remove from oven, reduce heat to 325°. Let dish stand for a few minutes. Stir in the cheeses and cream. Return to oven, bake 10–15 minutes longer, being careful not to let soup boil.

Serves 4–6.

JO STALLARD

Printed by permission of Gilroy Garlic Festival Association, Inc. Copyright © 1980, 1982 by Celestial Arts, P.O. Box 7327, Berkeley, CA 94707

WHEN **Louis Moran** brought his Tamale recipe backstage, it sounded simple enough. But it took on a new meaning when we learned that a few years ago he had no money and ingeniously came up with 101 different kinds of tamales. Now he employs over 300 people and well deserves to be called "Mr. Tamale."

Tamale

2 pounds beef, pork or chicken, diced
3 tomatoes, chopped
1 onion, chopped
¼ bell pepper, chopped
1 green chili, chopped
¼ teaspoon cumin
¼ bushel cilantro
 Salt and pepper to taste
2 packages California chili pepper
1 package hot New Mexico chili pepper
1 8-ounce package corn husks
1 5-pound package masa harina

In a large pot, place beef, pork or chicken; tomatoes; onion; bell pepper; green chili; cumin; cilantro and salt and pepper. Cook until meat is tender, approximately 35–40 minutes. Drain the liquid from meat mixture into a bowl, and add mixed chili peppers to liquid. Stir. Combine meat mixture and chili pepper mixture, cook 20 minutes and let marinate in refrigerator 3–4 hours. Soak corn husks in water to cover for 2 hours. Drain.

To assemble tamale, take one of the corn husks, spread thin layer of masa harina on the husk. Fill husk with meat and chili pepper mixture. Then roll husk around the meat and fold narrow end toward the middle. When all husks have been filled with the mixture, place them open end up on a rack over boiling water in a steamer. Cover and cook for 35 minutes, or until tamales feel lightly firm. Serve with Mexican rice and beans.

Makes 35–40.

Louis Moran
"Mr. Tamale"

CERTAIN names are synonymous with cooking. **Craig Claiborne's** is one. He made his recipe for Indian Keema with Peas, and frankly, I just watched a master at work and loved every minute of it! Craig's written many cookbooks, and naturally, when we invited him to the *Hour* kitchen, we felt we were entertaining true royalty! I really love it when I get a chance to watch and listen to a king of the culinary arts.

Indian Keema with Peas

1 tablespoon peanut, vegetable or corn oil
¾ cup finely chopped onion
1 tablespoon finely minced garlic
1 tablespoon finely minced or grated fresh ginger
1 tablespoon curry powder or paste
½ teaspoon ground cinnamon
½ teaspoon ground turmeric
½ teaspoon ground coriander
½ teaspoon ground cumin
1 pound ground lean meat, such as beef, lamb or veal
1 cup chopped, unsalted tomatoes, fresh or canned
1 tablespoon lime juice
  Salt to taste (optional)
1 teaspoon granulated sugar
  Freshly ground pepper to taste
¼ teaspoon crushed hot red pepper flakes (optional)
1 cup peas, fresh or frozen

Heat the oil in a heavy skillet and add the onion and garlic. Cook, stirring, until onion is wilted. Sprinkle with ginger, curry powder, cinnamon, turmeric, coriander and cumin. Stir to blend. Add the meat. Cook, stirring and chopping down with the side of a heavy metal spoon to break up any lumps. When the meat has lost its raw look, add the tomatoes, lime juice, salt and sugar. Add a generous grinding of pepper and the hot red pepper, if desired. Cover closely and let simmer for 30 minutes. Add the peas and continue cooking until peas are tender. If frozen peas are used, they need only to be heated through. Fresh peas might require 5 to 10 minutes cooking time. Serve with rice, and cucumbers with yogurt or mint with yogurt.

Serves 4.

CRAIG CLAIBORNE

ARGENTINE cooking—ever tried it? **Chris Better** was born and raised in Argentina, came to Los Angeles and opened up a restaurant called REGINA'S. She brought us her recipe called Cuscinetto. It's an unusual entrée, and the taste is worth the effort.

Cuscinetto

1 slice eggplant, ½ inch thick
1 egg, beaten
Bread crumbs
Fat for deep frying
2 tablespoons marinara sauce
Salt and pepper to taste
4 ounces filet mignon
2 thin slices cooked ham (picnic)
2 slices mozzarella cheese

Preheat broiler. Take slice of eggplant, dip in beaten egg and then in bread crumbs. Deep fry until crispy on the outside. Season marinara sauce to taste. Grill or broil the filet mignon to taste. Remove meat from heat, put 1 tablespoon marinara sauce on top of meat. On top of sauce, put eggplant, 1 more tablespoon sauce, and the ham on top of that. Cover completely with mozzarella cheese. Put under preheated broiler until cheese melts and becomes golden on top. Serve with a favorite vegetable.

Serves 1.

CHRIS BETTER

Printed by permission of Regina's Restaurant.

J OAN Nathan, author of cookbooks that cover Jewish cuisine from ancient traditions to modern techniques, presented her Friday Night Brisket on the show. She remarked that the use of so much garlic is typical, and reminded us of the words in the Talmud encouraging Jews to eat garlic on Friday. Why? According to Joan, in the ancient world garlic was believed to be an aphrodisiac, and a husband is supposed to fulfill his marital obligation to his wife—at least on Friday night. Joan told me she serves this brisket with noodles, and when she makes it for Hanukkah she serves it with potato pancakes and applesauce.

Friday Night Brisket

1 4-pound brisket
6 cloves garlic, crushed
Salt and pepper to taste
Paprika to taste
2 tablespoons vegetable oil
2 large onions, chopped
6 carrots, chopped
4–5 stalks celery with leaves, chopped
1 cup water, tomato juice or tomato sauce
1 envelope dried onion soup

Preheat oven to 325°. Rinse the meat with water. Pat it dry. Rub the meat on all sides with crushed garlic and then sprinkle with salt, pepper and paprika. Heat the oil in a heavy-bottomed casserole, and brown the meat on all sides. Add the onion, carrots and celery. Cover meat with water or tomato juice or tomato sauce and sprinkle with the dried onion soup. Cover and bake in the oven for 3 hours. Before serving, remove lid and brown ½ hour more. This dish is best prepared a day in advance so the fat is easily skimmed off before the brisket is reheated.

Serves 6–8.

JOAN NATHAN

Reprinted by permission of Schocken Books, Inc., from *The Jewish Holiday Kitchen* by Joan Nathan. Copyright © 1979 by Schocken Books, Inc.

Steak à la Stone

```
 4 large slices onion
 2 whole pimientos
   Butter
   Olive oil
16–18 ounces sirloin steak
 2 pieces toast
   Melted butter
   Parsley, chopped
```

Preheat broiler. In a frying pan, sauté onion and whole pimientos in butter
and a touch of olive oil. Sauté for 3 minutes. Put aside while you broil the
steak. When it's done, slice at an angle and place on the toast. Spread onions
and pimientos on top. Pour melted butter and parsley over that. So much for
Steak à la Stone.

Serves 1.

WALLY GANZI, JR.

Printed by permission of Palm Restaurants.

Lemon Ginger Beef

```
¾ pound flank steak
 1 tablespoon cornstarch
```

1 tablespoon dry sherry
2 tablespoons peanut oil
1 clove garlic, minced
  Lemon Ginger Sauce (see below)
1 cup thin, diagonally cut carrot slices
1 medium onion, cut into chunks
1 16-ounce can Del Monte cut green beans (no salt added),
    drained, liquid reserved
1 cup sliced fresh mushrooms

Lemon Ginger Sauce

3 tablespoons fresh lemon juice
1 tablespoon dry sherry
1 clove garlic, minced
2 tablespoons honey
1 tablespoon slivered ginger root
1 teaspoon cornstarch

Slice meat in thin bite-size pieces, cutting across the grain. Combine with cornstarch, sherry, 1 tablespoon oil and the garlic. Marinate 30 minutes.

Prepare Lemon Ginger Sauce by combining all ingredients and mixing well; set aside. Prepare all vegetables. Heat wok or skillet. Add remaining 1 tablespoon oil. Stir fry meat 2 to 3 minutes, or until just cooked. Remove from pan; set aside. Add carrot and onion to pan. Stir fry 2 minutes. Add 1 tablespoon bean liquid. Cover and steam 2 minutes, or until carrots are tender crisp. Add drained beans, mushrooms and Lemon Ginger Sauce. Bring to boil; cook, stirring constantly, until sauce is thickened and translucent. Add meat; heat through. Serve over unsalted cooked rice, if desired.

Note

May be accompanied by a salad of spinach leaves, cherry tomato halves, bean sprouts, sliced green onion and cilantro, tossed with your favorite low-sodium oil-and-vinegar dressing.

Serves 4.

DONNA HIGGINS, DEL MONTE CORP.

Lamb Chops with Mint Butter

2 tablespoons chopped fresh mint leaves, *or* 1 tablespoon dried
1 stick (½ cup) unsalted butter, softened
¼ teaspoon salt
Freshly ground pepper to taste
1 teaspoon lemon juice
3 loin lamb chops, 1½ inches thick, *or* 6 thin rib lamb chops

In food processor or blender, combine the mint, butter, salt, pepper and lemon juice until smooth. Chill about 10 minutes, or just until firm enough to roll into a cylinder about 2 inches in diameter. Wrap in waxed paper and chill additional 10 minutes. Slice into medallions.

With sharp knife score lamb chops on both sides. Place a medallion of mint butter on each chop and let chops stand for 30–40 minutes at room temperature. Preheat broiler.

Broil the chops for 8–10 minutes, turning at least twice. Serve directly from the broiler onto individual plates.

Serves 3.

MARTHA STEWART

M UU Shu Pork is a favorite of mine, but naturally I've only eaten it in Chinese restaurants. **Rhoda Yee,** who left her native China at the age of twelve and is now living in San Francisco and teaching dim sum cooking, taught me that Muu Shu Pork (or chicken) can actually be made at home by any cook who enjoys a challenge.

Muu Shu Pork

Peking Doilies (see recipe below)
Green onions (For onion brushes, see *Note*, p. 38)

Meat Marinade

1 teaspoon cornstarch
2 teaspoons dark soy sauce
1 teaspoon sherry

½ pound pork, cut the size of match sticks
4 Oriental dried mushrooms
¼ cup cloud ears
24 lily buds

Sauce

1 tablespoon cornstarch
2 tablespoons oyster sauce
1 teaspoon sesame oil
1 teaspoon sherry
1 teaspoon light soy sauce
¼ cup chicken broth

2 tablespoons oil, approximately
1 cup bean sprouts
1 cup bamboo shoots, cut the size of match sticks
2 cups Napa cabbage, shredded
2 green onions, cut into ½-inch lengths
¼ cup hoisin sauce

Prepare Peking Doilies as directed below. Cool, wrap and store in refrigerator until needed. Prepare onion brushes (see *Note*, p. 38).

Mix ingredients for meat marinade and marinate pork for ½ hour. Soak mushrooms, cloud ears and lily buds until soft. Discard mushroom stems and cut caps into thin slices. Tie a knot in the middle of each lily bud and nip off tough ends. Pinch off tough parts of cloud ears before breaking them into small pieces. Combine sauce ingredients.

Place 1 teaspoon oil in wok or skillet and stir fry bean sprouts for 1 minute. Remove from pan and set aside. Add 1 teaspoon oil to pan and stir fry bamboo shoots and cabbage for 2 to 2½ minutes. Set aside. Add 1 tablespoon oil and stir fry pork, mushrooms, lily buds and cloud ears until pork is done, about 2–3 minutes. Add sauce mixture, stirring until thickened. Return bean sprouts, bamboo shoots and cabbage to pan, and add the green onions.

Serve with steamed Peking Doilies (see directions below). You will need onion brushes and ¼ cup hoisin sauce. Spread a little hoisin sauce on a doily with the tip of the onion brush and spoon on Muu Shu Pork. Wrap and eat as a finger food.

Note

To make onion brushes, wash and cut green onions, white and light green parts, into 1½-inch lengths, one for each person. Slash ends repeatedly to a depth of ½ inch, to make very fine brushes, and soak in ice water for a few hours. Drain.

Peking Doilies

½ cup plus 4 teaspoons boiling water
2 cups all-purpose flour, sifted
¼ cup sesame oil (or vegetable oil)

Mix boiling water with flour and knead dough for 10 minutes. Let dough rest for 10 minutes. Break into 12 pieces. Roll each piece into a ball, then flatten with the heel of your hand. Brush half of the rounds with sesame or vegetable oil. Top each with another, unoiled, round. Roll each double round into a 6–7-inch pancake.

Heat a Teflon or heavy-bottomed skillet, without oil, over medium heat. Cook doilies for 1 minute or less on each side. They should turn a light beige. Cool for several seconds but separate each pair of doilies as soon as possible while still hot.

These can be cooked in advance and frozen for 1–2 months. There is no need to separate them with waxed paper. Steam frozen doilies for 12 minutes or, if thawed, steam for 6–7 minutes.

Tips

The following points should be observed to make successful doilies:

The dough should be a bit on the dry side—*too* dry and the doilies will crack—but they definitely should not be so soft as to become too mushy for rolling and separating. You should oil the flattened dough well, especially the edges, in order to have an easier time pulling them apart.

Roll doilies out away from the center in one stroke in each direction to ensure evenness and a round shape. Don't roll with a back-and-forth motion, since the edges may fold in, making the doilies difficult to separate.

A tortilla press would be a help. Before you begin rolling the doilies out (they're a bit slippery because of the oil in between the rounds), press them in the tortilla press. This will help you get started much more quickly.

Makes 12 doilies; serves 4–6.

RHODA YEE

I love French cooking, and as a matter of fact, I can even read the menu in French restaurants. But to tell you the truth, I can hardly pronounce the dish that **Chef Michel Yhuelo,** of LE DOME restaurant in Los Angeles, prepared in *Hour*'s kitchen. As I recall, though, the taste was *magnifique!*

Choucroute Alsacienne (Sauerkraut Garnished with Meat)

 7 ounces rendered pork or goose fat
 3 large onions, finely diced
 3 large cloves garlic, peeled
 2 pounds salt pork
 5 pounds fresh sauerkraut, washed and well drained
 1 pound thick-sliced bacon
 4 pigs' knuckles
20 juniper berries
 2 bay leaves
   Salt and pepper
 2 quarts water
 2 Polish garlic sausages
 8 smoked pork chops
 8 potatoes
 8 frankfurters or knockwurst

Preheat oven to 400°. Melt fat in a heavy 8-quart Dutch oven or deep roasting pan. Sauté onions until golden; remove and set aside. Insert whole garlic cloves into salt pork.

Place a third of sauerkraut in pan. Layer with half each of the salt pork, bacon, knuckles and onions. Combine 10 juniper berries and 1 bay leaf in each of two cheesecloth bags; place one bag atop layered ingredients. Add salt and pepper to taste. Repeat layers, beginning with sauerkraut, and second cheesecloth bag and top with remaining third of the sauerkraut. Add 2 quarts water. Cover and cook 3 hours. (Oven is preferred to top of range for more even dispersal of heat.)

After 3 hours, slice garlic sausage into 8 pieces. Arrange with pork chops on top of sauerkraut. Cover and continue cooking for 30 minutes. Taste for seasoning. Meanwhile, steam the potatoes and boil the frankfurters.

To serve, arrange sauerkraut in a dome shape on a large platter, discarding seasoning bags. Place meats attractively atop sauerkraut. Remove salt pork if desired. Arrange potatoes around edge of platter, or serve from separate vegetable bowl. Accompany with an assortment of mustards, coarse French bread, Gewürztraminer and beer.

Serves 8.

CHEF MICHEL YHUELO

Printed by permission of "Le Dome" Restaurant, Los Angeles.

PICTURE the perfect chef—dignified but friendly—whose very presence makes you willing to savor anything he cooks. You've imagined the extraordinary **Chef Louis Szathmáry**. THE BAKERY RESTAURANT, which he opened in 1953, is a Chicago landmark. Educated as a journalist and psychologist, he's been an actor, soldier, marriage counselor, lecturer and author, and today is known internationally simply as Chef Louis.

Roast Pork with Hungarian Sausage

1 piece Hungarian or Polish sausage, approximately ⅔ inch
in diameter and as long as the pork loin
2–4 pound pork loin, center cut

1 medium-size onion, skin on
1 small carrot
1 rib celery
1 quart water
2 cloves garlic, chopped
2 tablespoons Chef's Salt
1 teaspoon caraway seeds, bruised

Straighten sausage by rolling tightly in foil. Place in freezer for at least 2 hours.

Remove all bones from pork loin except rib bones. Cut off fat part from top. Reserve fat. With long, thin-bladed knife, carefully make a hole through the entire length of the pork loin. Keep to the middle as much as possible. (You may want to ask the butcher to do this preparation for you.)

Preheat oven to 350°. Slice onion (including skin), carrot and celery, and place in bottom of roasting pan. Pour water over vegetables. Add garlic. Cut fat trimmed from pork loin into ¼-inch cubes. Fry them until they turn dark brown.

Rub Chef's Salt into surface of the whole top of the roast, bottom of ribs and the two ends. Rub in caraway seeds. Carefully insert stiffly frozen sausage into pork loin, starting at one end of roast and gently pushing it in, turning it from side to side. It will help if you first insert a wooden-spoon handle slightly smaller than diameter of sausage. Place pork, rib side down, on vegetables and pour the smoking hot fat over top. Cover pan. Roast 1½–1¾ hours, or until meat thermometer registers 165°–175°. Baste every 15–20 minutes.

Remove roast from oven. Place on serving platter. Let stand in a warm place for at least 30 minutes. Strain liquid from vegetables. Skim fat from the juices. Place juices in a small saucepan over medium heat. Reduce them to a third the original amount. Serve as a clear sauce.

Note

If you prefer a country pork gravy, reduce liquid to half. Combine 1 cup milk and 2 tablespoons flour and add 4–5 drops of Kitchen Bouquet. Stir this mixture into the simmering pan juices.

Serves 4–6.

CHEF LOUIS SZATHMÁRY

Printed by permission of Chef Louis Szathmáry. Copyright © 1981 by Louis Szathmáry, published by C.B.I. Publ. Co.

Poulet au Kari à la Crème
(Chicken Breasts in Curried Cream Sauce)

1¾ pounds skinless, boneless chicken breasts
2 tablespoons butter
   Salt and freshly ground pepper to taste
¼ cup finely chopped shallots
1 tablespoon curry powder, or more to taste
½ cup dry white wine
1¼ cups heavy cream

Trim around the chicken breasts to cut away and discard the fat and membranes. Cut the chicken into strips about ½ inch wide. Melt the butter in a skillet and, when it is quite hot but not brown, add the chicken. Sprinkle with salt and pepper. Stir often until the chicken strips lose their raw look, about 2 minutes. Sprinkle the chicken with the shallots and curry powder. Stir well to blend and cook about 1 minute. Transfer the chicken to a bowl.

Add the wine to the skillet and cook over high heat for about 3 minutes, or until it is reduced to ¼ cup. Add any juices that have accumulated in the bowl containing the chicken. Add the cream to the skillet, and cook over high heat for about 4 minutes. Add the chicken and stir to blend well. The chicken must be piping hot throughout. Serve with hot rice, or Riz au Sultan (see below).

Riz au Sultan
(Rice with Raisins and Pine Nuts)

2 tablespoons butter
3 tablespoons finely chopped onion
½ teaspoon finely minced garlic
1 cup uncooked rice
¼ cup raisins
1½ cups chicken broth
¼ cup pine nuts

Melt 1 tablespoon of the butter in a saucepan and add the onion and garlic. Cook, stirring, until wilted. Add the rice, stir. Add the raisins. Add the chicken broth and bring to a boil. Cover and let simmer exactly 17 minutes. Add the pine nuts and remaining butter. Stir to fluff the rice while blending in the nuts.

Serves 4.

PIERRE FRANEY

Reprinted by permission of The New York Times Company. Copyright © 1981 by The New York Times Company.

DEDE Napoli, the mother of two male college students, decided, since she couldn't be with them while they were living on campus, to write a cookbook for them with easy-to-prepare, economical and nutritious recipes. Voilà, you have *The Starving Students Cookbook*. And now you will understand this Chicken on a Diet.

Chicken on a Diet

1 frying chicken, cut up
Salt and pepper to taste
1 can orange soda
¼ cup soy sauce

Preheat oven to 325°. Wash chicken (remove skin), and dry on paper towels. Salt and pepper chicken and place in foil-lined broiler pan. Mix together orange soda and soy sauce. Pour over chicken. Bake for 1 hour, or until chicken is tender. Spoon sauce over chicken a couple of times while cooking.
    Great to nibble on next day.

Serves 2–4.

DEDE NAPOLI

Reprinted by permission of Dede Napoli, author of *The Starving Students Cookbook*, © 1982 by Dede Napoli and published by Warner Books.

LEMON Chicken sounds ordinary. However, when **Titus Chan,** the remarkable chef and educator, prepared it onstage, it tasted tangy and unique. If you check the ingredients, you'll find that the marinade and sauce give it that special flavor that separates the chef's recipes from the novice's.

Lemon Chicken

4 chicken breasts, *or* 1 fryer, cut up

Marinade

2 teaspoons cornstarch
1–2 teaspoons sesame oil
1–2 teaspoons sherry or wine
¼ teaspoon salt
Dash white pepper

Sauce

2 teaspoons cornstarch
3 teaspoons water
⅓ cup water
⅓ cup cider vinegar
⅓ cup brown sugar, packed
¼ teaspoon yellow food coloring
1 lemon, cut in thin circles

Batter

1 egg
1 teaspoon water
2 teaspoons oil
½ cup cornstarch

4–6 cups vegetable oil for deep frying

Debone and score the chicken. Mix together all ingredients for marinade and marinate chicken for ½ hour.

To make sauce, mix 2 teaspoons cornstarch with 3 teaspoons cold water in small bowl. Place the remaining sauce ingredients in a saucepan and bring to boil. Gradually stir in cornstarch-water mixture to form a rich yellow sauce. Simmer 5 minutes.

Beat egg lightly with a fork, then combine with the 1 teaspoon water, 2 teaspoons oil and ½ cup cornstarch to make a batter. Add chicken to batter. Coat completely. Then deep fry 7–8 minutes, or until chicken floats and is a rich golden color. Drain, blot dry; salt, if desired. Cut into 1 x 2-inch pieces and cover with sauce. Serve immediately.

Serves 4.

TITUS CHAN

Printed by permission of Titus Chan, author of the *Aloha China Cookbook*, published by Oriental Cookbook Publishers.

BORN and raised in Sri Lanka, off the coast of India, **Christine Harrison** has been in America for over ten years, importing and marketing spices. She cooked Tandoori Chicken for us. Its flavor proves "The Spice Lady" is a name Christine truly lives up to!

Tandoori Chicken

1 3-pound chicken, cut up
8 ounces plain yogurt
2 teaspoons salt
1 teaspoon pepper
1 teaspoon ground cumin
1 teaspoon paprika
1 teaspoon ground ginger
3 cloves garlic, crushed
2 tablespoons lime juice

Remove skin and trim fat from chicken pieces. With a knife, make deep slits into the meat. In a large bowl, mix yogurt, salt, pepper, cumin, paprika, ginger, crushed garlic and lime juice. Add chicken to the yogurt mixture, mix until well coated. Cover and refrigerate for 8 hours, or overnight.

Preheat oven to 425°. Arrange chicken on baking sheet and bake for 40 minutes, or until fork tender.

Serves 6.

CHRISTINE HARRISON
"THE SPICE LADY"

PETER **Prescott** is associate editor of Food and Wine magazine. He not only writes about entertaining stylishly at home, but also is responsible for the overall "look" of that magazine. He visited Hour's kitchen and brought a recipe for chicken with cognac.

Breast of Chicken Charente

4 chicken breasts, skinned and boned
½ cup all-purpose flour
1 tablespoon dried tarragon
2 tablespoons salt
4 tablespoons unsalted butter
½ cup cognac
1 cup chicken broth
4 tablespoons Dijon-style mustard
2 tablespoons lemon juice
4 tablespoons capers

Split the chicken breasts lengthwise. On a sheet of waxed paper, combine the flour, tarragon and salt. Lightly dredge the chicken breasts in the mixture, shaking off the excess.

In a large skillet, melt the butter over moderate heat. Add the chicken and sauté for 5–7 minutes, or until lightly browned on each side. In a small saucepan, over moderate heat, warm the cognac. Pour it over the chicken and ignite, shaking the pan constantly until the flames subside. Add the chicken broth, mustard and lemon juice. Cover the skillet, reduce the heat to low and simmer for 20 minutes, turning the chicken breasts once.

Arrange the chicken breasts on a warmed platter. Using a fine sieve, strain the sauce over the chicken and sprinkle with the capers.

Serves 4.

PETER PRESCOTT

WOK cooking is an art in itself. Expert Chinese chef **Stephen Yan** says, "Chinese cooking is like making love! It takes a very long time to prepare, but the actual cooking time is very short." Try his Chicken Slices with Pineapple, and keep that concept in mind.

Chicken Slices with Pineapple

¾ pound chicken meat, sliced
½ teaspoon Chinese cooking wine
1 teaspoon light soy sauce
3 green onions, cut into 1-inch lengths
½ teaspoon minced garlic
½ teaspoon minced ginger
  Sesame oil
1 small green pepper, cut in squares
1 small red pepper, cut in squares
8 ounces pineapple chunks
¼ teaspoon salt
1 tablespoon cornstarch
¼ cup water
½ tablespoon soy sauce
  Pinch of sugar

Marinate chicken in the Chinese cooking wine and light soy sauce, mixed together. Heat wok, brown green onion, garlic and ginger in a few drops of sesame oil; add chicken and sauté until meat changes color. Put in all vegetables, sprinkle with ¼ teaspoon salt, and stir fry for 4 minutes. When chicken is done, make sauce mixture of cornstarch, water, ½ tablespoon soy sauce, pinch sugar and a few drops of sesame oil. Add to chicken and bring to a boil. Mix well and serve with rice.

Serves 2–3.

STEPHEN YAN

EXOTIC Middle Eastern cooking ... sound complicated? **Rose Dosti,** author of *Middle Eastern Cooking,* explained that Bastela is a national dish in Morocco and is served at banquets and on important occasions. It's brought to the table on huge brass or silver trays, and guests use their fingers to break off the filo pastry. She suggests that, for your next party, you serve this at a low table and seat your guests on high pillows. Count me in!

Bastela Morocco (Chicken Pastry)

1 2–2½ pound chicken, cut up
  Salt and freshly ground black pepper to taste
2 tablespoons peanut oil
1 medium onion, chopped
2 cups chicken broth or water
  Pinch of saffron threads or powder (optional)
1 cinnamon stick
½ cup fresh chopped parsley
½ cup chopped cilantro
6 eggs, beaten
2 cups ground toasted almonds
¼ cup granulated sugar
½ teaspoon ground cinnamon
¼ cup clarified butter
7 filo pastry sheets
¼ cup confectioners' sugar
  Ground cinnamon for garnish
  Kumquats for garnish (optional)

Place chicken in a large skillet. Sprinkle with salt and pepper. Pour peanut oil over chicken. Add onion and broth or water. Stir in saffron, if desired. Bring to a boil. Add cinnamon stick. Reduce heat and cover. Simmer over low heat 1 hour, or until chicken is very tender. Remove chicken from skillet. Reserve liquid.

When chicken is cool, remove meat from bones. Shred chicken into bowl. Set aside. Remove cinnamon stick from skillet and discard. Measure 1 cup liquid and return to skillet. Bring to boil. Add parsley, cilantro and eggs, and cook until scrambled and liquid is absorbed. Set aside. Combine almonds, granulated sugar, ½ teaspoon ground cinnamon in small bowl. Set aside.

Preheat oven to 350°. Butter a 10-inch pie plate or ovenproof skillet with rounded sides. Stack filo pastry sheets. Cover with plastic wrap to prevent drying out. Place 4 filo sheets in bottom of skillet, brushing each with clarified butter. Allow a 5–6-inch overhang. Sprinkle a third of the almond mixture over filo sheets. Top with half the shredded chicken. Top with another third of the almond mixture. Drain egg mixture, if necessary. Place half the egg mixture over almond mixture. Repeat until all ingredients are used, ending with almond mixture. Fold overhang over filling. Smooth down creases. Brush with butter. Top with remaining 3 filo sheets, brushing each with butter and folding overhang under. Bake 25–35 minutes, or until golden brown. Cool slightly. Invert onto a platter. Sprinkle with confectioners' sugar. Make a decorative crisscross design with cinnamon. Garnish with kumquats, if desired. Cut in wedges and serve hot.

Serves 5–6.

ROSE DOSTI

Printed by permission of Rose Dosti. Copyright © 1982 by H P Books.

CHICKEN in Phoenix Nest ... sound too difficult? **Chef Chu** shows us how to go about preparing it successfully. The flavor makes it worth the trouble!

Chicken in Phoenix Nest

The Phoenix, which represents beauty and grace, is properly commemorated in the presentation of this dish. Cubes of plump chicken nestle in a lacy basket made of shredded potato. Green pepper, slices of carrot and delicate quail eggs are a colorful and surprising addition.

    1 large russet potato
      Water
      Pinch salt
    1 broiler-fryer chicken (about 2½ pounds), boned, skinned
        and cut into bite-size pieces
    2 teaspoons light or regular soy sauce
    2 teaspoons dry sherry
    1 egg white
    1 tablespoon cornstarch
    1 tablespoon vegetable oil
    ½ teaspoon cornstarch
    2 quarts vegetable oil for deep frying
   12 tablespoons soy sauce

1 tablespoon dry sherry
2 tablespoons hoisin sauce
2 green onions (white part only), finely chopped
1 clove garlic, sliced
1 green pepper, seeded and cut into 1-inch squares
¼ white onion, cut into 1-inch squares
6 thin slices carrot
Dash sesame oil
5–6 quail eggs
Shredded lettuce or bok choy

Peel potato and shred; place in a bowl of water, add salt and let stand until ready to use. Combine chicken with 2 teaspoons soy sauce, 2 teaspoons dry sherry, the egg white, 1 tablespoon cornstarch and 1 tablespoon vegetable oil, in the order listed; set aside and let stand for 10 minutes. Drain potato thoroughly and toss with the ½ teaspoon cornstarch. In a wok, heat 2 quarts oil to 350°.

To shape nests, dip two identical medium-size wire strainers into the hot oil to prevent sticking, and distribute half the potato evenly around the sides and bottom of one strainer. Press the other strainer down into the potato-lined one. Holding the strainers tightly together, carefully lower them into the oil and rotate so that oil touches all the sides. Deep fry potato nest for 3–4 minutes, basting if necessary, until it becomes slightly brown. Remove from oil, gently separate strainers and tap nest out onto a paper towel to drain. Repeat, using remaining potato.

To oil-blanch chicken, remove 1 quart oil from wok (reserve for future use), and heat remaining oil to 300°. Add chicken, stirring to separate, and blanch for 2–3 minutes. Remove and drain. Set aside. Combine 2 tablespoons soy sauce, 1 tablespoon dry sherry and the hoisin sauce, and set aside.

To stir fry vegetables, remove all but 3 tablespoons oil from the wok and, when hot, add green onion and garlic. Stir fry until fragrant, and then add green pepper, white onion, carrot and chicken. Cook for 1 minute; stir in hoisin sauce mixture. Continue cooking and stirring for 1 minute longer, then stir in sesame oil and drained quail eggs.

To serve, position potato nests on platter lined with shredded lettuce or bok choy. Fill each nest with half the chicken mixture, carefully keeping quail eggs on top.

Serves 4–6.

CHEF LAWRENCE CHU

I F you love to cook, but hate to clean all those messy pots, you'll appreciate **Annette Annechild**'s suggestions for using your wok. Author of *Getting Into Your Wok,* Annette found a way to combine turkey leftovers with the indispensable tamari sauce to create a healthful entrée.

Wokked Turkey Cashew

¼ cup tamari or soy sauce
2 tablespoons cornstarch
½ teaspoon salt
  Peanut oil for cooking
1 head broccoli, cut into bite-size pieces
1 bunch scallions, chopped
8 ounces fresh mushrooms, sliced (or substitute canned, sliced)
  Leftover turkey, cut in strips (2 cups)
1 4-ounce package cashews
1 cup stock (chicken, turkey or vegetable)
  Hot cooked brown rice or leftover stuffing

Mix together tamari or soy sauce, cornstarch and salt in small bowl; set aside. Heat wok and necklace with oil. Add broccoli and stir fry until almost tender. Add a little more oil, if necessary, and then add the rest of vegetables. Stir fry 3 minutes. Add turkey slices and cashews, and stir fry 1 minute. Add stock, cover and simmer 1 minute. Add tamari-cornstarch mixture and cook until sauce thickens, stirring constantly. Simmer 1 minute, uncovered, and serve over rice, or next to warmed stuffing.

Serves 4.

ANNETTE ANNECHILD

Elegant Poached Filet of Sole

½ cup pineapple juice
1 cup white grape juice, or more as needed
½ teaspoon ground ginger
2 teaspoons lemon juice
2 pounds filet of sole
1 cup purple grapes, halved and seeded
1 kiwi fruit, peeled and sliced
1 cup unsweetened pineapple chunks

In a large skillet, bring pineapple juice, grape juice, ginger and lemon juice to a boil. Add sole, reduce heat, and poach fish until it flakes, about 8 minutes. If liquid doesn't cover fish, add more grape juice. Remove fish from poaching liquid carefully, using two spatulas to avoid breaking filets. Garnish with grapes, kiwi fruit and pineapple.

Serves 4–6.

PRESENTED BY TOM NEY

Reprinted by permission of Rodale Press, Inc., Emmaus, PA 18049, from *Rodale's Basic Natural Foods Cookbook,* © 1984 by Rodale Press, Inc.

POISSON du Lac Bourguignon ... are you ready for this? I was confident, because next to me stood **Jeff Fields,** the owner of the famous Malibu restaurant, LES ANGES. But go ahead, try your hand at it and let me know what happens!

Poisson du Lac Bourguignon

2 7-ounce filets of fresh pike

Fish Stock

2 pounds raw fish bones from pike or any other white fish
4 ounces carrots

4 ounces leeks
4 ounces celery
Bay leaf
Sprinkle each of rosemary and thyme

2 medium-size russet potatoes, peeled
3 green onions, white part only
1–2 thick strips of bacon
½ bottle of red Burgundy
2 cups fish stock
2 tablespoons sweet butter
Salt, pepper

Bone pike filets. To prepare stock, put fish bones, carrots, leeks and celery in a saucepan; cover with water and add bay leaf, rosemary and thyme. Boil uncovered for 15 minutes. Strain. Set aside.

Cut potatoes into quarters and carve into large olive-size shapes. Peel green onions, cutting away dark green part. Steam potatoes and onions until cooked but firm. Set aside.

Cut bacon into 2-inch strips. Sauté until crispy. Set aside.

In saucepan, reduce wine by half. Add fish stock and reduce to 1 cup. Add 1 tablespoon sweet butter to smooth the sauce. Add salt and pepper to taste. Reserve while preparing fish.

In a separate pan, sauté the fish filets in the remaining butter, cooking the fish for approximately 4 minutes on each side. Remove and place on serving plates, adding the sauce. Garnish with the green onions, potatoes and bacon strips.

Serves 2.

PRESENTED BY JEFF FIELDS

Pan-fried Trout with Homemade Herb Breading Mix

Homemade Herb Breading Mix

½ cup all-purpose flour
½ teaspoon salt
1 teaspoon paprika
1 teaspoon garlic powder
½ cup grated Parmesan cheese
1 teaspoon lemon-and-pepper seasoning mix
½ teaspoon dried sweet basil
¼ teaspoon onion powder

6 pan-size trout, dressed
1 cup Homemade Herb Breading Mix
1 stick (½ cup) butter
1 lemon
¼ cup chopped fresh parsley (or substitute dried)

At home, combine ingredients for breading mix and store in plastic containers in your refrigerator. Take along when camping to use for breading trout or other fresh-caught fish. Makes 1 generous cup breading mix; sufficient for 6 pan-size trout.

Wash and clean trout. (*Note:* If trout are somewhat damp, breading mix will adhere more easily.) Place breading mix in a small paper bag. Place one trout at a time in bag and shake around so that fish is fully coated; repeat with all trout.

Melt butter in a large skillet. Add trout to hot melted butter and cook over medium to high heat for about 3 minutes, or until browned on first side. Turn trout to second side and squeeze lemon juice on top. When trout has browned on second side, about another 3 minutes, garnish with chopped parsley; serve.

Note

Breading mix is also delicious with chicken, veal or pork.

Serves 3–6. (Remember, on camping trips, appetites increase!)

KAREN GREEN

WHAT happens when a nice Jewish girl from Japan moves to New York City? Well, I guess she opens up a kosher Japanese restaurant called SHALOM JAPAN! **Miriam Mizakura** did just that, and came to our studios to present one of her popular dishes, Marinated Salmon!

Marinated Salmon

  1 2½-pound salmon filet
  6 cups sake
1½ cups granulated sugar
  2 teaspoons soy sauce
  3 cups rice vinegar
  5 cups fish stock
  2 teaspoons salt

Slice salmon. In large, deep skillet, heat sake. Ignite fumes with match (this removes alcohol). Add remaining ingredients to skillet; add salmon slices. Cook for 5 minutes. Remove salmon and continue cooking liquid until it thickens into sauce. Place salmon on plate and top with sauce. Chill.

Serves 6–8.

MIRIAM MIZAKURA

> L E ST. GERMAIN was the first of the new breed of French restau-
> rants to open in Los Angeles, starting a trend that's still growing.
> Co-owner Chef **Paul Bruggemans** visited the *Hour* kitchen. Below is
> a recipe for Baked Salmon with Caviar and Chives that is currently
> being served at Le St. Germain. Just reading the ingredients makes
> my mouth water!

Baked Salmon with Caviar and Chives

4 7-ounce pieces of filet of salmon
Pinch of black pepper
½ glass dry white wine
1 tablespoon red wine vinegar
Juice of ½ lemon
1 bay leaf
Pinch salt
2 shallots, chopped
2 tablespoons heavy cream
2½ sticks (1¼ cups) sweet butter, cut in small pieces
1 ounce Beluga caviar
4 tablespoons fresh chopped chives

Preheat oven to 450°. Get a frying pan with ovenproof handle very hot on top of stove, and, without any fat, sauté the pieces of salmon ½ minute on each side. Place frying pan in oven for 4 minutes; the salmon is ready.

Place pepper in a saucepan with white wine, wine vinegar, lemon juice, bay leaf, salt and chopped shallots; reduce liquid by three-quarters. Add cream, bring to a boil ½ minute. Add butter one small piece at a time and whisk until sauce is slightly thickened, then put through a fine strainer. Add caviar and chives.

Place a piece of salmon on each of four plates. Pour sauce over salmon and serve with steamed vegetables. A very dry white wine would complement the dinner.

Serves 4.

PAUL BRUGGEMANS

Printed by permission of Le St. Germain Restaurant.

Peruvian Causa

2 13-ounce cans light tuna or albacore chunk, water packed
1 large red onion, coarsely chopped
   Mayonnaise
¼ cup lemon juice
3 tablespoons red wine vinegar
   Salt and pepper to taste
4 pounds russet potatoes
⅓ cup vegetable oil
2 tablespoons lemon juice
1 head Boston lettuce
2 hard-boiled eggs, sliced
1 avocado, sliced
24 black olives, pitted

Drain tuna; mix with onion and enough mayonnaise to hold together. Season with ¼ cup lemon juice, red wine vinegar, salt and pepper. Refrigerate. This is your salad mixture.

Cook potatoes, whole in their skins, until soft. Peel and mash while still hot. Add salt to taste. Let cool. Add vegetable oil and 2 tablespoons lemon juice. Work like dough, with your hands. Divide potato mixture into two equal parts. Form first half into a layer and place on a round platter. Spread tuna mixture over layer and top with second half of potatoes. This should look like a cake, ready to be frosted. Cover entire Causa with thin layer of mayonnaise. Garnish all around with lettuce. Top with egg and avocado slices and black olives. I usually put a tomato rose on the top for color.

Serves 6–8.

PILAR WAYNE

Seafood Gumbo II

½ cup salad oil
½ cup all-purpose flour
1 large onion, chopped
2–3 cloves garlic, minced
1 1-pound can tomatoes, undrained
1½ pounds frozen okra, or equivalent
Oil for frying okra
2 quarts hot water
3½ tablespoons salt
¾ teaspoon red pepper
1 large bay leaf
¼ teaspoon thyme
8–10 allspice berries
Few grains chili pepper
2 pounds headless raw shrimp, fresh peeled
1 pound claw crab meat, picked
1 pint oysters
½ cup chopped green onions
½ cup chopped parsley
Hot cooked rice

In a large heavy pot, make a very dark roux of the salad oil and flour. Add onion and garlic. Cook slowly until onion is transparent. Add tomatoes and cook on low heat until oil rises to the top (about 30 minutes), stirring frequently. In separate skillet, fry okra in oil over moderately high heat, stirring constantly until okra is no longer stringy. Add the okra to the mixture in the pot, stir and simmer about 10 minutes. Add hot water, salt and red pepper. Simmer partially covered for 45 minutes. Add other seasonings and simmer an additional 20 minutes; then add shrimp and simmer 15 minutes. Add crab meat and simmer 15 minutes more. Add the oysters for the last 5 minutes of cooking. Taste carefully for seasoning, adding more if necessary. Remove from heat and stir in green onions and parsley. Serve over rice. Variations may be made by adding different seafoods, sausages or poultry.

Serves 8–10.

DONNA SAURAGE

THE Cajun King himself, **Paul Prudhomme,** graced *Hour*'s kitchen more than once. He gave me a tip I'll never forget: The same ingredient put into the recipe at different times can give you extremely different tastes! (Please don't scowl if *you* knew that.) I'll tell you, I listen to anything Paul Prudhomme says about cooking. This chef and owner of one of America's most famous restaurants, K-PAUL'S LOUISIANA KITCHEN, knows what cooking is *all* about!

Garlic Shrimp with Oysters on Pasta

2 quarts hot water
1 tablespoon salt
1 tablespoon vegetable oil
½ pound fresh spaghetti, *or* ⅓ pound dried
Oil for tossing spaghetti
1½ sticks (¾ cup) unsalted butter, *in all*
½ cup chopped green onions
8 peeled medium shrimp (about 3 ounces)
1 tablespoon minced garlic
Seasoning Mix (see below)
¾ cup warm seafood stock
8 shucked medium oysters, drained (about 5 ounces)

Seasoning Mix

¾ teaspoon salt
½ teaspoon sweet paprika
½ teaspoon white pepper
½ teaspoon dried thyme leaves
½ teaspoon onion powder
¼ teaspoon black pepper
½ teaspoon ground red pepper (preferably cayenne)

Combine hot water, salt and oil in large pot over high heat, cover, bring to a boil. When water reaches rolling boil, add spaghetti, small amounts at a time, breaking up oil patches as you drop it in. Return to boil and cook, uncovered to al dente stage (about 4 minutes for fresh spaghetti, 7 minutes for dried); do not overcook. During this cooking time use a wooden spoon to lift spaghetti up by spoonfuls and shake strands back into boiling water. Immediately drain spaghetti into colander; stop its cooking by running cold water over strands. (If you used dry spaghetti, first rinse with hot water to wash off starch.) After spaghetti has cooled, about 2–3 minutes, pour liberal amount of vegetable oil in hands and toss spaghetti. Set aside in the colander.

Heat serving plate in a 250° oven. Combine Seasoning Mix ingredients thoroughly in a small bowl, set aside. Melt 6 tablespoons of butter in a large skillet over high heat. Add green onions, shrimp, garlic and Seasoning Mix; cook until shrimp turn pink, while vigorously shaking pan in a back-and-forth motion (rather than stirring) for about 1 minute. Add oysters, stock and remaining 6 tablespoons butter. Cook about 1 minute until butter melts and oysters curl, continuing to shake pan. Add spaghetti; toss and cook spaghetti until just heated through. Remove from heat and serve.

For each serving, roll spaghetti on a large fork and place on heated serving plate. Top with remaining sauce and garnish with the shrimp and oysters.

Note

The sauce for this dish is best if made only 2 servings at a time. If you want to make more than 2 servings, do so in separate batches, but serve while piping hot.

Serves 2.

PAUL PRUDHOMME

Reprinted by permission of William Morrow & Company from *Chef Paul Prudhomme's Louisiana Kitchen*. Copyright © 1984 by Paul Prudhomme.

ONE of the legends in California cuisine is the Austrian-born chef, **Wolfgang Puck.** He was chef and co-owner of the famed Los Angeles bistro MA MAISON and is now the owner of two new posh and very popular restaurants in Los Angeles, SPAGO and CHINOIS. With all this fanfare and success, he is still delightful and unassuming, as personable as he is talented.

Chinese Lobster

1 tablespoon Chinese black beans
⅓ cup sake
⅓ cup chicken stock
1 tablespoon soy sauce
2 teaspoons minced fresh ginger
1 1–1½-pound lobster
1 tablespoon dark sesame oil
2 scallions, sliced thin
½ bunch Chinese garlic (garlic chives), minced
1 teaspoon cornstarch, dissolved in 1 tablespoon sake

Soak the black beans in the sake, chicken stock, soy sauce and ginger for an hour or so. Preheat the oven to 400°. To kill lobster, turn it on its back and insert a sharp knife between body and shell at tail to sever spinal cord, or plunge head first into boiling water for 5 minutes. Heat the sesame oil in a sauté pan large enough to hold the lobster. When the oil is very hot, sauté the lobster briefly on both sides to coat it with oil. Cook in the oven for 10 to 12 minutes, or until bright red.

Remove the lobster from the sauté pan. Set aside to cool for a few minutes. When it cools enough to handle, remove the top shell in one piece and reserve it. Cut the underside into quarters, leaving the legs attached. Deglaze the pan with the bean-sake mixture. Add the scallions, Chinese garlic and cornstarch. Add the quartered lobster and toss over moderate heat until the sauce thickens enough to adhere to the lobster.

On a large heated plate, reassemble the lobster quarters to approximate original appearance. Place reserved upper shell over the legs so the lobster is reconstituted. Spoon remaining sauce over lobster. Serve immediately.

Serves 1–2.

WOLFGANG PUCK

NICK Montoya, chef at DON SALSA's in El Monte, California, famous for their margaritas and great Mexican food, came on the show to share his recipe for Mariscos Supremo and a side dish of Iced Avocado. It turned out to be one of the more memorable Mexican fiestas!

Mariscos Supremo

2 whole 1½-pound Eastern lobsters, cooked
2 tablespoons butter
2 tablespoons olive oil
6 raw jumbo shrimp, peeled and deveined
4 ounces raw scallops
2 ounces sliced onion
½ ounce fresh garlic, chopped
2 ounces sliced bell pepper
4 ounces fresh mushrooms, sliced
2 ounces chopped parsley
8 ounces cooked crab
3 ounces diced fresh tomatoes

Sauté Marinade

2 tablespoons sherry
1 tablespoon lemon juice
6 tablespoons chicken broth
1 tablespoon Worcestershire sauce
½ ounce garlic
Salt and freshly ground pepper to taste

Sliced avocado
Tomato slices
Lemon wedges

Extract lobsters from shells. Set aside. Reserve shells to decorate serving platter, if desired. In a sauté pan, heat butter and oil to sizzling. Add shrimp and scallops, sauté for 30 seconds. Continue adding, in order, onion, garlic, bell pepper, mushrooms, parsley. As shrimp becomes milk white and firm, add lobster, crab and tomatoes. Cook until heated. Mix together ingredients for Sauté Marinade. Add to sauté pan and swirl gently. Serve on heated platter. Garnish with sliced avocado, tomato slices and lemon wedges. Serve with Iced Avocado (see below).

Iced Avocado

1 avocado, peeled and seeded
1 cup chicken broth
4 tablespoons sour cream
2 tablespoons dry sherry
¼ teaspoon crushed garlic
  Dash Worcestershire sauce
¼ teaspoon Poupon mustard
½ teaspoon lemon juice
  Dash red wine vinegar
5 drops olive oil
  Salt and pepper to taste

Mash avocado. Add all other ingredients. Thin to desired consistency with additional chicken broth. Serve on ice.

Serves 6.

CHEF NICK MONTOYA

WHAT happens when you combine pasta, asparagus, mush-rooms, cauliflower, zucchini and carrots in a Chinese wok? You get an all-time favorite—Pasta Primavera. **Rita Leinwand** presented this entrée, and if you try it you'll discover why it was such a success on *Hour Magazine* and backstage!

Pasta Primavera

½ stick (¼ cup) unsalted butter
1 medium onion, minced
1 large clove garlic, minced
1 pound thin asparagus, tough ends trimmed, cut diagonally into ¼-inch slices, tips left intact

½ pound mushrooms, thinly sliced
6 ounces cauliflower, broken into small flowerets
1 medium zucchini, cut into ¼-inch-thick rounds
1 small carrot, halved lengthwise, cut diagonally into ⅛-inch slices
1 cup low-fat yogurt or heavy cream
½ cup chicken stock
2 tablespoons chopped fresh basil, *or* 2 teaspoons dried
1 cup frozen tiny peas, thawed, *or* 1 cup fresh young peas (see *Note*)
2 ounces prosciutto or cooked ham, chopped
5 green onions, chopped
Salt and freshly ground pepper to taste
1 pound fettuccine or linguine, cooked al dente, thoroughly drained
1 cup freshly grated imported Parmesan cheese

Heat wok or large, deep skillet over medium-high heat. Add butter, onion and garlic, and sauté until onion is softened, about 2 minutes. Mix in asparagus, mushrooms, cauliflower, zucchini and carrot, and stir fry for 2 minutes. (At this point, remove several pieces of asparagus tips, mushrooms and zucchini, and reserve for garnish.) Increase heat to high. Add yogurt or cream, stock and basil, and allow mixture to boil until liquid is slightly reduced, about 3 minutes. Stir in peas, ham and green onion, and cook 1 minute more. Season to taste with salt and pepper. Add pasta and cheese, tossing until thoroughly combined and pasta is heated through. Turn onto large serving platter and garnish with reserved vegetables. Serve immediately.

Note

Vegetables may be chopped several hours in advance, wrapped and refrigerated.

Frozen tiny peas tend to be sweeter than fresh peas from the market. If using peas from your garden, shell just before adding to wok with asparagus and other vegetables. For a variation add 1 pound cooked, shelled shrimp with peas and ham.

Serves 4–6.

RITA LEINWAND

T HEY lecture around the country together, they work together, they play together, they cook together, they eat together! When you talk about marital stews in the von Welanetz family, you're probably just talking about another great meal! **Diana and Paul von Welanetz** are authors and chefs extraordinaire. On one of their visits to *Hour*'s kitchen, they made a pasta that's as beautiful to look at as it is to eat.

Pasta Tricolore

We named this dish after the Italian flag because of its distinct white, green and red colors.

Sauce

⅔ cup "extra-virgin" olive oil
2 medium cloves garlic, minced
2 large bunches fresh basil, leaves only, minced
½ bunch parsley, leaves only, minced
½ medium-size red (Bermuda) onion, minced
5 large ripe tomatoes, seeded and diced
2 teaspoons coarse salt
¾ teaspoon freshly ground black pepper
1½ pounds dried pasta of your choice, *or* 3 (12-ounce) packages frozen tortellini, cooked

Combine the sauce ingredients in a serving bowl, cover and leave at room temperature for at least 1 hour to blend the flavors. Just before serving, cook the pasta according to package directions until barely tender and still chewy (al dente). Drain well and toss immediately with the sauce. Any leftovers can be refrigerated to serve as a pasta salad the next day.

Note

The sauce will only improve if allowed to marinate for several hours at room temperature. If necessary, the sauce ingredients, except for the tomatoes, can be assembled a day or two ahead of time and stored in the refrigerator. Several hours before serving, bring to room temperature and add tomatoes.

Serves 6–8.

DIANA AND PAUL VON WELANETZ

Reprinted by permission of Jeremy P. Tarcher, Inc., from *The von Welanetz Guide to Ethnic Ingredients* by Diana and Paul von Welanetz. Copyright © 1982 by Diana and Paul von Welanetz.

I met **Sophie Kay** in Milwaukee, Wisconsin, on a television show where she had been cooking up a storm for thirteen years. I invited her to *Hour Magazine*'s kitchen so we could taste her delectable Zucchini Pasta.

Zucchini Pasta

10 ounces fresh zucchini, cubed
½ cup boiling water
2 large eggs, at room temperature
1 tablespoon vegetable oil
4 cups all-purpose flour, white or unbleached
2 teaspoons granulated sugar
1 teaspoon salt

Cook zucchini in ½ cup boiling water until tender; drain. Puree in blender with 1 egg and the vegetable oil. Make a well in the flour. Break the remaining egg into well. Add sugar and salt. Beat mixture in the well with a fork, about 10 strokes. Add zucchini puree to well, and beat before working in the flour. Continue beating until dough becomes sticky and difficult to work with the fork. Knead by hand to make a rough-looking dough. Let dough rest 10 minutes. Knead until most of the flour is used and dough is smooth and elastic, about 10 minutes. Divide dough into 3 or 4 balls and place balls in a plastic bag; set aside to rest 30 minutes before rolling by hand. Roll out one ball at a time to desired thickness and cut into desired shape and width.

Serves 8.

Plain Pasta

3 cups all-purpose flour, white or unbleached
¾ cup plus 2 tablespoons water
1 teaspoon salt

Place flour in a mound on a large flat surface. Make a well in the center. Add water and salt. Using a fork, gently start to work flour from the side of the well into the liquid mixture. Continue as directed for Zucchini Pasta.

Serves 6.

SOPHIE KAY

TALIAN music, good wine and pasta ... What more could you ask for? Chef **Franco Frachey** came to *Hour Magazine* and prepared Spaghetti all' Ubriacone. If you follow his recipe carefully, you'll create a flaming pasta in the process. Frachey is a pro, but it looked relatively easy anyway. So I suggest you try your hand at it too—carefully.

Spaghetti all' Ubriacone

¼ pound smoked ham, chopped
1 cup coarsely chopped onion
½ cup chopped carrots
½ cup chopped celery
3 tablespoons butter
¾ pound ground beef
2 tablespoons olive oil
1 cup dry red wine
2 tablespoons tomato sauce
2 cups beef stock
¼ pound chopped chicken livers
1 cup heavy cream
  Nutmeg, salt and pepper to taste
1 pound thin spaghetti
¾ cup scotch whisky
  Parmesan cheese, grated

Combine ham, onion, carrots and celery on a cutting board. Chop finely. (Mixture is called *battuto*.) In a heavy skillet, melt the butter over moderate heat. When foam subsides, add battuto and cook for 10 minutes until slightly browned. In a separate skillet, brown ground beef in olive oil. Stir constantly, breaking up meat chunks. Add red wine and increase heat. Continue stirring until liquid evaporates. Add tomato sauce and beef stock to mixture. Reduce heat, cover and simmer for 45 minutes, stirring occasionally. Brown chicken livers in battuto and butter. Cook 3–5 minutes. Add livers, battuto and cream to meat mixture. Add seasonings to taste. Meanwhile, cook spaghetti in boiling water for 6–7 minutes. Drain spaghetti. Pour whisky into skillet in which battuto was cooked and ignite, burning away the alcohol. Add spaghetti and sauce. Toss spaghetti and add Parmesan cheese.

Serves 6.   FRANCO FRACHEY

PAT McMillen, senior producer of the *Donahue* show, was forced to develop a do-it-ahead method of cooking in order to balance career and family. She's the author of *The Working Woman's Cookbook & Entertainment Guide,* and besides tasting her Irish Spaghetti, during her visit we found out what was *really* cooking on *Donahue.*

Irish Spaghetti

2 cups elbow macaroni
4–6 cups water
1 tablespoon butter, margarine or oil
½ teaspoon salt
1 pound ground beef
½ cup chopped onion
2 16-ounce cans peeled tomatoes, chopped, with liquid
1 cup tomato juice
4–5 teaspoons granulated sugar
1 tablespoon butter or margarine
Salt and pepper to taste

To cook the macaroni, put the water, 1 tablespoon butter and ½ teaspoon salt in a large saucepan, and bring to boil. Add elbow macaroni, return to boil, and cook, uncovered, 8–10 minutes, stirring occasionally. Drain well and set aside.

Put ground beef and onion in frying pan, and cook over medium heat, breaking up ground beef with wooden spoon, until beef is browned. Drain and put meat mixture in saucepan large enough to hold all ingredients. Add tomatoes with their liquid; tomato juice; sugar; 1 tablespoon butter; cooked, drained macaroni; salt and pepper to taste. Stir to mix well and bring to boil over high heat. Lower heat and simmer, stirring occasionally, 10–15 minutes longer. Serve immediately.

Note

This can be served as is, or it can be turned into a buttered baking dish and baked in 350° oven 30–45 minutes.

Serves 4–6.

PAT MCMILLEN

THE famous butcher **Merle Ellis** educated millions of people about the fine art of buying meat and stretching your dollar at the meat market through his popular television and syndicated newspaper series. Of course, with meat prices soaring, Merle Ellis is the best friend a cook ever had!

Cassoulet

1½ cups dry white navy, great northern or white kidney beans
¼ cup cooking oil
1 tablespoon salt
  Water
  Bones from pork loin roast
2 strips bacon, cut up
½ pound Italian hot sausage or other hot sausage, cut into pieces
¾ cup chopped onion
½ cup diced celery
¼ cup diced carrot
1 clove garlic, minced
1 tablespoon chopped parsley
1 bay leaf
1 tablespoon rosemary, crushed
¾ cup white wine
1 13-ounce can (1½ cups) chicken broth
¼ cup toasted bread crumbs

Combine beans, oil, salt and water to cover beans. Soak overnight.

Drain beans; discard water. Cut excess fat from pork bones. In pressure cooker, sauté bacon and sausage until browned. Remove from pan. Brown pork bones in fat and remove from pan. Pour off excess fat. Put soaked beans into pan; add vegetables, seasonings, wine and chicken broth. Place bacon, sausage and bones on top of beans. Close pressure-cooker cover securely. Place pressure regulator on vent pipe. Cook for 30 minutes at 15 pounds pressure. Turn off heat. Let pressure drop of its own accord. Remove pork bones; cool slightly. Remove any meat scraps from bones and add to beans. Sprinkle toasted bread crumbs over beans; stir mixture gently to distribute meat and crumbs.

Serves 4–6.

MERLE ELLIS

THE dictionary defines "vegetarians" as those who eat no meat or fish. And **Judi and Shari Zucker,** identical twins and authors of *How to Eat Without Meat: Naturally,* are proof that it's a healthful idea.

Eggplant Parmesan

1 large eggplant
6 large tomatoes, or tomato sauce (about 10 ounces)
2 cloves garlic, minced
1 teaspoon basil
  Dash of mixed Italian herbs
  Pat of butter (optional)
1 pound mozzarella cheese, thinly sliced or shredded
½ cup sliced green olives
  Parmesan cheese, grated

Preheat oven to 375°. Peel eggplant and slice crosswise into ½-inch slices. Soak in water for 20 minutes, then drain. Blend the tomatoes in an electric blender with the minced garlic, the basil and a dash of mixed Italian herbs (or basil and marjoram), or mix garlic and herbs with tomato sauce. Butter casserole or baking dish, if you wish, and make successive layers of eggplant, mozzarella, tomato puree and sliced olives, ending with top layer of Parmesan cheese. Bake for 45–50 minutes.

Variation

Dip slices of eggplant in a mixture of 1 or 2 beaten eggs, ½ cup yogurt, ½ cup water, and pat on each side in a shallow pan containing ¾ cup bread crumbs. Layer in casserole or baking dish and bake as directed above.

Serves 6.

JUDI AND SHARI ZUCKER

A potato knish. Simple, nutritious, and in no time at all you'll agree with **Alice Kadish** from My Mother's Knish: "You haven't eaten . . . until you've eaten my mother's knish," says she. Hmm . . .

Potato Knish

4–6 potatoes, cooked and peeled
Margarine (optional)
Fresh fried minced onion to taste
Salt and pepper to taste
Favorite pastry or dough recipe, or filo dough or frozen
    pastry dough from supermarket or bakery
1 egg beaten with a little water (egg wash)

Preheat oven to 375°. Mash potatoes, adding margarine, if desired. Mix in fried onion and salt and pepper to taste. Roll dough out into 4 x 4-inch squares. With an ice-cream scoop, place filling on each square. Fold corners in to middle, turn over, place knish on baking sheet. Slit each knish with a knife and brush with egg wash. Bake for 20–25 minutes.

Note

For variety, add dry cottage cheese or cooked, chopped chicken, beef or liver to basic potato filling!

Makes 8–12.

ALICE KADISH

Printed by permission of My Mother's Knish.

I F you're one of those people who has an aversion to tofu, an increasingly popular import from the Orient, you should really reconsider. Tofu's nutrients make it well worth acquiring a taste for it. The authors of **Nikki and David Goldbeck**'s American Whole Foods Cuisine just might be able to win you over with their recipe for Tofu à la King.

Tofu à la King

¾ pound frozen tofu
1 cup cold water
2 tablespoons soy sauce
2 tablespoons butter
1 medium onion, chopped
¼ cup chopped green pepper
2 cups dried mushrooms
¼ cup whole-wheat flour
1½ cups milk
½ cup chopped pimiento
3 tablespoons dry sherry
Dash hot pepper sauce
2 biscuits, toast slices or muffins per serving

Unwrap tofu, place in a bowl, cover with boiling water. Let stand while preparing remaining ingredients. (When tofu is defrosted, drain and squeeze dry.)

Combine 1 cup cold water and soy sauce. Marinate tofu. Soak mushrooms to soften. Melt butter in 1½-quart saucepan, sauté onion, green pepper and drained mushrooms for 5 minutes, or until soft. Stir in flour, gradually add milk. Cook over medium heat, stirring frequently, until thick. Drain tofu, squeeze out moisture. Tear tofu into small pieces. Add tofu, pimiento, sherry and hot pepper sauce to sauce, and cook for 5 minutes. Serve over bread base.

Serves 4–6.

NIKKI AND DAVID GOLDBECK

N O innovation has appealed to a busy homemaker more than the microwave oven. **Grace Wheeler** has been teaching microwave cooking classes and serving as a consultant to oven manufacturers for over ten years. Recent studies indicate that the microwave oven *is* a superior way to cook fruits and vegetables, because less water and up to 70 percent less cooking time is needed. As a result, fewer nutrients are heat damaged or lost to cooking water. So why not try one of Grace's healthful recipes for vegetables.

Fresh Vegetable Medley

Fresh Vegetable Medley takes on a new dimension when cooked in the microwave. Take note of the vegetables' superb texture and color retention.

       2 medium-size bunches of fresh broccoli (about 1½ pounds)
       2 small zucchini or crookneck squash
      12 medium-size fresh mushrooms
       1 small carrot, peeled and sliced very thin diagonally
     2–3 tablespoons butter or margarine (optional)
          Seasoning to taste
       2 small tomatoes (optional)

Cut broccoli into flowerets; save the stems for another use. Slice squash into ¼-inch-thick slices; slice mushrooms or leave whole. Arrange vegetables on a platter suitable for the microwave oven, placing broccoli around outside edge, then the squash, and the mushrooms in the center. Tuck carrot slices among the broccoli flowerets. If using butter or margarine, melt in a small custard cup about 20 seconds, and drizzle over vegetables. Season lightly. Cover platter with plastic wrap, sealing edges to keep in steam. (*Note:* No water is being added.) Cook in microwave oven on full (100 percent) power 8–10 minutes, or until just crisp tender. Remove plastic wrap carefully, so as not to be burned by steam. Cut tomatoes into wedges, if using, and arrange over vegetables. Season tomatoes. Return to microwave oven and cook on full power for 1½–2 minutes, or until tomatoes are heated through.

Food for thought: It is important to slice the carrots thin so that they will become tender.

Serves 6–8.

GRACE WHEELER

Printed by permission of Grace Wheeler from *Microwave Cooking My Way*. Copyright © 1978 by Rand Editions, Leucadia, CA.

IF you cook every day, the idea of making something different is always appealing. **Jennifer Brennan,** author of *Cuisines of Asia* and *The Original Thai Cookbook,* showed us how you can, with patience and perseverance, reproduce the exotic tastes of Thai food.

Navrattan Pilau
(Multicolored Rice with Panir, Tomatoes, Peas and Nuts)

        9 ounces Patna or Basmati rice
        4 tablespoons ghee (clarified butter)
      ½ medium onion, thinly sliced
        6 cloves garlic, chopped
      12 whole black peppercorns
        6 whole cloves
        1 1-inch stick cinnamon
        1 1-inch piece ginger, minced
        6 whole green cardamom seeds (with husks)
     1½ teaspoons ground cumin
        2 green chilies, seeded and finely chopped
     1½ teaspoons salt
        6 drops green food coloring mixed with 1 tablespoon
            water
      ½ cup cooked green peas
      ¼ teaspoon salt
      ¼ teaspoon white pepper
        4 drops red food coloring mixed with 1 tablespoon water
        1 large tomato, seeded and diced
      ¼ teaspoon red chili powder (cayenne)
      ¼ teaspoon salt
      ¼ teaspoon garam masala
   ⅛–¼ pound panir, diced into ½-inch cubes and quickly fried
            in ghee (Feta or other hard, curd cheese may be sub-
            stituted for panir)
      ¼ teaspoon salt
      ¼ teaspoon white pepper

Core

        4 tablespoons ghee
        1 ounce unsalted cashews
        1 ounce almonds, blanched and skinned
        1 ounce unsalted pistachio nuts, shelled
        ¼ cup sultanas (large golden raisins)
        2 green serrano chilies, seeded and slivered
        1 1-inch piece ginger, thinly sliced
        4 ounces slivered onions, fried crisp in ghee (ready-made
             dried onion flakes may be substituted)
        ¼ teaspoon salt
        ¼ teaspoon chili powder
        2 hard-boiled eggs, chopped

        Parsley or coriander leaves, for ganish

Wash rice thoroughly and soak for about 30 minutes. Heat 4 tablespoons ghee in large, heavy saucepan and fry sliced onion and the garlic until onion becomes translucent. Add the peppercorns, cloves, cinnamon stick, minced ginger, cardamom, cumin, chopped green chilies and 1½ teaspoons salt to the onion and garlic. While mixture is frying, drain rice, reserving the water. Add rice to ingredients in saucepan and fry it, stirring constantly, until translucent. Now add rice water, about 1½ cups, to the frying rice. (Increase water proportionally if larger amounts of rice were originally used.) Increase heat to high and bring the mixture to a boil. Cover, reduce heat and simmer until all moisture is absorbed and rice is cooked and firm. When rice is cooked, remove cover and let steam escape. Remove from heat and set aside to cool, stirring occasionally to separate the grains. Discard whole spices.

Divide cooked rice into thirds and place in 3 medium-size saucepans. Use the green food coloring to color rice in one pan green, stirring in the peas, ¼ teaspoon salt and ¼ teaspoon white pepper. Color rice in next pan red, stirring in red food coloring and adding the tomato, ¼ teaspoon chili powder, ¼ teaspoon salt and the garam masala. Leave rice in remaining pan "white," but stir in the panir, ¼ teaspoon salt and ¼ teaspoon white pepper. Cover the 3 pans and place them over a very low heat for about 10 minutes to allow rice to absorb the coloring.

Heat the 4 tablespoons ghee for the Core in a medium frying pan over medium-high heat, and fry the nuts, sultanas, serrano chilies and sliced ginger, stirring, until sultanas begin to puff up. Add the onions or onion flakes, reduce heat to low and add the salt, chili powder and eggs. Cook the Core mixture until eggs are just warmed through.

Now for the Fun Part!

In the center of a heated platter, place the egg-nut Core in a shallow mound. One by one, carefully spread the three colors of rice in layers over top of mound and platter. Sprinkle top layer with chopped parsley or coriander leaves, and serve at once. (Navrattan Pilau usually accompanies a mutton curry.)

Serves 4–8.

JENNIFER BRENNAN

MORE vegetables . . . more complex carbohydrates . . . more wok cooking. **Sharon Wong Hoy** showed us how quickly you can put together stir-fried vegetables.

Stir-fried Vegetables with Baby Corn

1 tablespoon oil
1 medium carrot, peeled and sliced diagonally
¼ teaspoon salt
½ onion, cut in ¾-inch squares
1 stalk celery, sliced diagonally
¼ teaspoon granulated sugar
1 cup canned straw mushrooms
1 cup canned baby corn, sliced in halves lengthwise
1 tablespoon oyster sauce
Dash of sugar
¼ pound Chinese pea pods
¾ cup chicken broth
1 teaspoon soy sauce
1 tablespoon cornstarch
1 tablespoon water
Salt and black pepper to taste

Heat oil in wok. Stir fry carrot for 30 seconds. Add ¼ teaspoon salt. Add onion and celery, and stir fry until crisp tender, about 45 seconds. Season with ¼ teaspoon sugar. Add mushrooms and baby corn, and stir fry 30 seconds. Add 1 teaspoon oyster sauce and dash of sugar.

Add pea pods, chicken broth, remaining oyster sauce and the soy sauce. Mix cornstarch with water and add. Season to taste with salt and pepper. Heat until gravy boils and thickens.

Serves 2.

SHARON WONG HOY

KEEP It Simple is the title of one of **Marian Burros'** cookbooks. She says that it's a book for people who care about food and themselves, but are in a hurry. The award-winning food editor of the *New York Times,* Marian Burros has offered us suggestions and advice for years and is one of the most outspoken consumer advocates in the country. Her Hot Potato and Broccoli Vinaigrette is a simple and nutritious addition to any meal.

Hot Potato and Broccoli Vinaigrette

    1 pound tiny new potatoes
    1 pound broccoli, tough stems trimmed off, heads cut into
        flowerets
    4 tablespoons cider vinegar
    4 tablespoons olive oil
    1 clove garlic, pressed or finely minced
    ½ teaspoon dry mustard
    ¼ teaspoon paprika
      Freshly ground black pepper to taste
    2 green onions, finely sliced, both white and green parts

Scrub potatoes and cook whole in their jackets in covered pot until tender, about 20 minutes. Cut in quarters. Steam broccoli over hot water until just tender, about 7 minutes. While potatoes and broccoli cook, make dressing. Combine remaining ingredients in a small saucepan and bring just to boiling; stir. Set aside. Place unpeeled, quartered potatoes and brocoli in serving dish and pour dressing over them. Stir gently and serve warm. (Amount of oil has been reduced by half.)

Serves 4.

MARIAN BURROS

ONE of the most renowned guests who ever cooked in *Hour*'s kitchen was the legendary **James Beard.** Truly, no one has had more influence on the American kitchen than Beard, who was seventy-eight when he appeared on our show to make his Hearty Beef Salad. Before his death he had published his twenty-fourth cookbook, called *The New James Beard,* and as always, his recipes brought cheers from all corners of the country. I was honored to cook with this great man.

Hearty Beef Salad

This beef salad is served as a first course in France, but is very satisfactory as a buffet, luncheon or supper dish.

> 2 cups boiled, sliced new potatoes
> 1 cup finely cut green onions
> 2 cups coarsely chopped celery, with leaves
> 3 cups lean boiled or pot-roasted beef, sliced and then cut in 1-inch squares
> 12 cornichons (French sour gherkins)
> 1 cup cherry tomatoes, *or* 4 peeled tomatoes cut in sixths
> ¼ cup capers
> 1 cucumber, peeled, seeded and diced
> ½ cup roasted and peeled green pepper strips
> Salad greens

Dressing

> 6 hard-boiled eggs
> 1 tablespoon Dijon mustard
> 1 cup olive oil
> 1 clove garlic rubbed into 1½ teaspoons salt
> 1 teaspoon freshly ground black pepper
> ⅓ cup wine vinegar
> Dash of Tabasco

Arrange the salad ingredients attractively on a bed of greens, either on a deep platter or in a large bowl. To make the dressing, shell the eggs, reserving the whites; mash the yolks with a fork and work in the mustard. Stir in the oil, garlic-flavored salt, pepper, vinegar and Tabasco. Pour dressing over the salad and garnish with the reserved egg whites, chopped.

Serves 6.

JAMES BEARD

Reprinted by permission of John Schaffner Assoc., Inc. Copyright © 1981 by Alfred A. Knopf.

> **J** EFF Smith, *The Frugal Gourmet* from the popular public television cooking series, came into *Hour*'s kitchen to prepare a delicate and unusual salad: Japanese Cucumber and Crab Salad. It was particularly tasty, so try it!

Japanese Cucumber and Crab Salad

Don't be put off by the salt; it is used to draw water from the cucumbers, and then the salt water is drained off.

    4 cucumbers, unpeeled, sliced thin
    1 tablespoon salt
    1 6-ounce can of crab meat
    ¼ cup light soy sauce
    ⅛ cup rice wine vinegar
    ½ tablespoon sesame oil
      Pinch of granulated sugar

Mix the cucumbers with salt. Place in a colander and drain for about 45 minutes. Mix with the crab. Make a dressing of the light soy sauce, rice wine vinegar, sesame oil and sugar. Toss with the cucumbers and crab, and serve.

Note

Light soy sauce, rice wine vinegar and sesame oil are available in any Oriental food store.

Serves 4–6.

JEFF SMITH

Reprinted by permission of William Morrow & Company from *The Frugal Gourmet* by Jeff Smith. Copyright © 1984 by Jeff Smith.

Pumpkin Seed and Date Bread

1¼ cups hulled raw pumpkin seeds
3 cups all-purpose flour
¾ cup finely snipped or chopped dates
2½ teaspoons baking powder
1 teaspoon baking soda
1½ teaspoons salt
1 cup regular or quick-cooking rolled oats
1½ teaspoons ground cinnamon
¾ teaspoon ground ginger
¾ teaspoon ground nutmeg
4 eggs, at room temperature
1 cup brown sugar, packed
½ cup vegetable oil
½ cup plain yogurt, at room temperature
1 16-ounce can pumpkin
Grated peel of 1 medium lemon

In a large skillet over medium heat, toast pumpkin seeds until they begin to make popping sounds and start to turn golden brown; set aside to cool. Grease two 8 x 4-inch loaf pans; set aside. Preheat oven to 350°. In a large bowl, combine flour and dates. Use your fingers to separate dates and coat with flour. Stir in baking powder, baking soda, salt, oats, cinnamon, ginger and nutmeg until combined; set aside. In medium bowl, lightly beat eggs. Stir in brown sugar, oil, yogurt, pumpkin and lemon peel. Stir into flour mixture until dry ingredients are just moistened. Stir in 1 cup toasted pumpkin seeds. Turn dough into prepared pans. Smooth tops; sprinkle 2 tablespoons toasted pumpkin seeds over top of each loaf. Lightly press into surface with back of spoon. Bake 60–70 minutes, or until a wooden pick inserted in center comes out clean. Let stand in pan 10 minutes. Turn out onto a rack to cool. Serve with Honey Butter (see below).

Makes 2 loaves.

Honey Butter

Naturally sweetened with honey, this creamy spread is delicious on almost any bread!

  ½ cup butter, at room temperature
  ⅓ cup honey
  ¼ teaspoon vanilla extract

In small bowl of electric mixer, or food processor fitted with metal blade, mix or process all ingredients until creamy. Spoon into small serving bowl. Cover and refrigerate. Let stand at room temperature 20 minutes before serving.

Variations

Cinnamon-Honey Butter: Add ½ to ¾ teaspoon ground cinnamon.
Honey-Berry Butter: Blot ½ cup minced fresh blueberries or strawberries on paper towels. Fold into honey butter.
Citrus-Honey Butter: Increase butter to ⅔ cup. Add 2 tablespoons lemon or orange juice and 2 tablespoons grated lemon or orange peel.

Makes about ¾ cup.

SHARON TYLER HERBST

Printed by permission of Sharon Tyler Herbst. Copyright © 1983 by H P Books.

Bananas Foster

2 tablespoons brown sugar
1 tablespoon butter
1 pound ripe bananas, cut in half and sliced lengthwise
Dash of ground cinnamon
2 tablespoons white rum
1 tablespoon banana liqueur
2 scoops vanilla ice cream

In a skillet or chafing dish pan, over medium heat, melt brown sugar and butter. Add bananas and sauté until tender. Sprinkle with cinnamon; keep warm. In a small saucepan, combine rum and liqueur; warm and set aflame. Stir to blend rum and liqueur into sauce until flame dies. Immediately pour over bananas. Serve hot over ice cream.

Serves 2.

MIRIAM LOO

Apple Tart

Sweet Dough

2 cups all-purpose flour
⅕ cup sweet butter

⅓ cup granulated sugar
2 egg yolks
Salt (optional)
2 tablespoons water

Apple Filling and Glaze

4 Golden Delicious apples
2 eggs
¾ cup granulated sugar
1 teaspoon vanilla
⅓ cup all-purpose flour
⅔ cup sweet butter

To make dough, mix flour with butter until powder fine. Add sugar, then beat two egg yolks (and salt, if desired) with water and add to flour-butter mixture. Mix until dough is formed. Wrap in plastic wrap and chill.

Preheat oven to 325°. Peel apples and slice very thin. Roll out dough and place in a 9-inch diameter double-bottomed tart pan, pressing dough well up on the side of pan. Arrange apples on top of dough. Beat eggs with sugar. Add vanilla and flour, and beat until smooth. Melt butter until golden brown, add to egg mixture and pour over apples. Bake at 325° for 60–75 minutes, or until dough and filling are cooked.

Serves 6.

ROGER BOURBAN
"LE GARÇON RAPIDE"

DEBORAH Kidushim-Allen has been a frequent guest on *Hour Magazine*. Besides preparing some unusual entrées and desserts, Deborah insists upon giving us calorie-, fat- and sodium-saving tips. It's a comfort to know, for instance, that each of these Greek nut-filled pastry rolls contains:

> 76 calories
> 0 sodium
> 4 grams fat
> 1 gram protein
> 8 grams carbohydrates
> 0 cholesterol

Makes you feel a little better about enjoying them, don't you think?

Bourma (Greek Nut-filled Pastry Rolls)

> ½ pound shelled pistachio nuts, walnuts or pecans, ground
> 1 tablespoon fructose
> ¾ teaspoon ground cinnamon
> 1½ tablespoons rose water
> 12 sheets (½ pound) phyllo dough
> ½ cup low-calorie margarine, melted

Rose Water Syrup

> 1 cup water
> ½ cup fructose
> 1 tablespoon fresh lemon juice
> 1 teaspoon rose water or rum extract

Preheat oven to 300°. In a mixing bowl, combine the nuts, 1 tablespoon fructose, cinnamon and 1½ tablespoons rose water. Set aside. Unroll the phyllo dough, remove 2 sheets and place on work surface. (Keep remainder of phyllo dough covered with waxed paper to prevent it from drying out.) Lightly brush the top sheet with margarine. Sprinkle about 2 tablespoons of the nut mixture over a lengthwise half of the phyllo. Place a wooden dowel, about ¾ inch in diameter and at least 24 inches long, along the nut-filled side of the phyllo sheets. Roll the phyllo loosely around the dowel. Lay the dough, seam side down, on work surface. Lift the ends of the dowel and, using your hands, gently push the dough together from each end to form a crinkled roll about 10 to 12 inches long. Slide roll off the dowel. Insert an index finger in each end of the roll to transfer it to a nonstick jelly-roll pan about 11 x 17 inches. (Or slide the crinkled roll off the dowel directly onto the pan.) Let stand uncovered so phyllo dries slightly while you make the remaining rolls. When all of the rolls are made and have dried slightly, pull the ends out accordion-fashion until they touch the 11-inch sides of the pan. Pour any remaining nut mixture over the top of the rolls, and bake in oven until lightly browned, about 35–40 minutes.

While the rolls are baking, make the Rose Water Syrup. Combine the water, fructose, lemon juice and rose water in a saucepan. Bring to a boil and cook to a syrupy consistency, about 20 minutes. Keep warm.

Remove the rolls from the oven and drain off any excess margarine from the pan. Using a serrated knife, immediately cut the rolls into pieces about 2 inches long. Pour warm syrup over warm pastries.

Calorie-, Fat- and Sodium-Saving Tip: Nuts are high in protein, but also very high in fat content. Pistachios have the lowest fat content and, as a result, the lowest calorie content. Avoid Brazil nuts as they have the most calories. Nuts are low in sodium if they are raw or dry roasted without added salt. Read labels to avoid hidden salt and fat.

Makes 36 pieces.

DEBORAH KIDUSHIM-ALLEN

Reprinted by permission of Harper & Row Publishers, Inc., from *Light Desserts Cookbook* by Deborah Kidushim-Allen. Copyright © 1981 by Debora Kidushim-Allen.

ABOUT nine years ago, **Debbie Fields** set out to make a better chocolate chip cookie. She came up with the famous Mrs. Fields Cookies. Naturally, she didn't give us her secret recipe, but she did give us one for a mocha pie, which, by the way, contains a pound of those extraordinary Mrs. Fields Chocolate Chip Cookies!

Mrs. Fields Mocha Pie

1 cup semisweet chocolate chips
½ stick (¼ cup) butter
1 cup heavy cream
1½ tablespoons instant espresso coffee powder
3 eggs, separated
¼ cup granulated sugar
1 pound Mrs. Fields Chocolate Chip Cookies

Topping

2 cups heavy cream
1 tablespoon granulated sugar
1 teaspoon vanilla, *or* ½ cup orange juice, freshly squeezed
½ cup semisweet chocolate chips, *or* grated rind of 1 orange

Preheat oven to 275°. In a heavy saucepan or top of a double boiler, melt together chocolate chips and butter. In a mixing bowl, whip 1 cup heavy cream until stiff and fold in coffee. In another bowl, beat egg whites until stiff and add ¼ cup sugar. Add egg yolks to chocolate mixture and stir until thick and well blended. Combine whipped cream-coffee mixture with egg white-sugar mixture, and fold in chocolate-yolk mixture until blended. Set aside.

Grind chocolate chip cookies in food processor. Spread crumbs in a 10-inch pie pan and place in oven for 10 minutes. Lay parchment paper, then a 9-inch pie pan on the crumbs in the 10-inch pie pan and press until crust binds together. Pour chocolate mocha filling into the cooled cookie pie crust. Refrigerate until time to serve.

To make topping, whip 2 cups heavy cream, add 1 tablespoon sugar; add 1 teaspoon vanilla, or ½ cup orange juice, and whip until stiff. Spoon over pie. Grate ½ cup chocolate chips in food processor and sprinkle over whipped cream peaks or, if using the orange juice, garnish with grated orange rind.

Serves 6.

DEBRA J. FIELDS

TOFFEE Chip Squares—even the name sounds wicked! **Jeri Dry** provided us with a recipe that made us deviate from our latest diets. But as I recall, it was well worth it!

Toffee Chip Squares

2 sticks (1 cup) butter
¾ cup brown sugar, packed
1 teaspoon vanilla
2¾ cups all-purpose flour
½ teaspoon baking powder
1 6-ounce package of semisweet chocolate chips
3 tablespoons butter
1 bag Butter Brickle

Preheat oven to 350°. Cream together 1 cup butter, the brown sugar and vanilla. Add the flour and baking powder, and mix. Pat the dough into an ungreased 8 x 8-inch pan and bake 15–18 minutes. Cut into 1-inch squares while hot; let cool.

In a saucepan, melt the chocolate chips. Add 3 tablespoons of butter. Using a pastry bag or spoon, put a drop of chocolate in the center of each cooled square. Toss some Butter Brickle on top of the chocolate while it's still warm. Refrigerate squares for about 1 hour to set.

Makes 64 squares.

JERI DRY, COOKIEMANIA

BESS **Hoffman** baked cookies, which actually raised money to help put her children through college. Now that's what I call making work fun! She made Cinnamon Logs/Cinnamon Swirls for us—just one of the recipes included in her extensive cookie-recipe book, *Cookies by Bess*.

Cinnamon Logs

2 sticks (1 cup) butter, slightly softened
1 teaspoon almond extract
1 tablespoon cinnamon
3 tablespoons granulated sugar
2 cups all-purpose flour
Granulated sugar

Preheat oven to 300°. Mix ingredients well, adding in order given. Shape dough in rolls about ½ inch in diameter. Cut in little logs about 1½ inches long. Bake on ungreased baking sheets for 25–30 minutes. Cool slightly. Roll in granulated sugar.

Makes about 80 small cookies.

Cinnamon Swirls

2 sticks (1 cup) soft butter
1 teaspoon vanilla
5 tablespoons granulated sugar
2 cups all-purpose flour
½ cup granulated sugar
½ teaspoon cinnamon

Preheat oven to 350°. Mix butter, vanilla and 5 tablespoons sugar. Divide flour into thirds, add one part at a time, mixing well, until all blended in. Using small star plate of cookie press, make swirls or wreaths on ungreased baking sheet. Bake for 15–20 minutes. While still hot, roll in mixture of ½ cup granulated sugar and the cinnamon. Transfer to rack to cool. Cookies freeze well.

Makes about 60 cookies.

BESS HOFFMAN

Oasis Oat Cookie

3–4 apples
4 teaspoons cinnamon
1 tablespoon honey
1 tablespoon lemon juice
4 egg whites
1 cup raw bran
½ cup oatmeal
½ cup powdered milk, noninstant and nonfat

Preheat oven to 350°. Quarter and core apples, leaving skin intact. Chop apples and sprinkle with cinnamon. Steam apples until tender, about 10 minutes. Cool and place in blender. Add honey, lemon juice and egg whites to blender, and puree. In a bowl, combine raw bran, oatmeal and powdered milk, and stir in apple mixture. Drop by teaspoonfuls on a nonstick cookie sheet. Bake for 20 minutes, or until brown and crisp. May be garnished with date sugar or date slivers.

Makes 32 cookies.

SHEILA T. CLUFF

Fig Pound Cake with Lemon Sauce

2 cups all-purpose flour
½ cup yellow cornmeal
½ teaspoon salt
2 sticks (1 cup) butter, softened
1⅔ cup granulated sugar
5 eggs
2 teaspoons vanilla extract
½ cup milk
1 cup dried calimyrna figs, chopped
½ cup pine nuts

Lemon Sauce

½ cup granulated sugar
1 tablespoon cornstarch
3 tablespoons fresh lemon juice
1 cup boiling water
2 tablespoons butter
Grated lemon rind
Salt to taste

Preheat oven to 350°. Butter and flour an 8 x 4 x 2-inch loaf pan. Combine flour, cornmeal and salt in bowl; stir with fork to mix well. Put 1 cup butter in a bowl, beat and slowly add the sugar, blend well. Add eggs to butter mixture, two at a time, and beat until light. Add flour mixture alternately with vanilla and milk; beat until smooth. Stir in figs and nuts. Spoon into loaf pan. Bake about 45 minutes, or until a straw inserted in center comes out clean. Cool on rack. Slice thin and serve with sauce.

To make sauce, combine the sugar, cornstarch and lemon juice in small pan. Add boiling water. Cook, stirring constantly, until thick and clear. Remove from heat. Stir in the butter, rind and salt to taste.

Variation

Omit figs and pine nuts from cake, substituting ⅓ cup chopped citron and 1 tablespoon caraway seeds.

Serves 16–20.

MARION CUNNINGHAM

EVERYBODY has heard of New York's celebrated "21" CLUB. **Jennifer Harvey** was the first woman chef to cook there. When she visited *Hour*'s kitchen, she brought along Chef Anthony Pedretti's famous recipe for "21" Club Rice Pudding—a pudding with style and class!

"21" Club Rice Pudding

1 quart milk
1 pint heavy cream
½ teaspoon salt
1 vanilla bean
¾ cup long-grained rice
1 cup granulated sugar
1 egg yolk
1½ cups whipped cream
   Raisins (optional)

In a heavy saucepan, combine the milk, cream, salt, vanilla bean and ¾ cup of the sugar, and bring to a boil. Stirring well, add the rice. Allow the mixture to simmer gently, covered, for 1¾ hours over a very low flame, until the rice is soft. Remove from the heat and cool slightly. Remove vanilla bean. Blending well, stir in the remaining ¼ cup of sugar and the egg yolk. Allow to cool a bit more. Preheat the broiler.

Stir in all but 2 tablespoons of the whipped cream; pour the mixture into individual earthenware crocks or a soufflé dish. (Raisins may be placed in the bottom of the dishes, if desired.) After spreading the remaining whipped cream in a thin layer over the top, place the crocks or dish under the broiler until the pudding is lightly browned. Chill before serving.

Serves 10–12.

JENNIFER HARVEY

Printed by permission of The "21" Club from *"21" The Life and Times of New York's Favorite Club* by Marilyn Kaytor, Viking, 1975.

R IMSKY KORSAKOFFEE is a desserts-only restaurant in Portland, Oregon. On a trip up north, Bonnie Strauss told me that she had an uncontrollable urge to visit this restaurant and meet the creator of these desserts, **Lizzie O'Rourke.** Lizzie, who hadn't ever had a cooking class, made Raspberry Zuccotto, using this adaptation of a traditional Italian recipe. I didn't get to taste this one, but when Bonnie told me about it, her expression said it all!

Raspberry Zuccotto

9 ounces (1 cup plus 2 tablespoons) soft butter
4 eggs
1½ cups granulated sugar
1 teaspoon grated lemon peel
2 cups sifted cake flour
1 quart heavy cream
½ cup confectioners' sugar
10 ounces raspberries
⅓ cup plus 3 tablespoons Grand Marnier
½ cup toasted almonds
6 ounces semisweet chocolate, melted and cooled
½ cup brandy or cognac

Preheat oven to 350°. Cream butter to the consistency of whipped cream. Set aside. In separate bowl, mixer on high speed, beat eggs, granulated sugar and lemon peel to the consistency of mayonnaise. On low speed, add flour until just incorporated. Fold in creamed butter, but don't overblend. Grease and flour a 9 x 5 x 3-inch loaf pan. Bake cake for 1¼ hours.

When the cake cools, take a 4-quart bowl, line with plastic wrap, slice pound cake into ¼-inch slices. Take 10 slices, cut diagonally. Lay diagonal slices in bottom of bowl, narrow points to center, edges overlapping slightly. Line rest of bowl with whole slices of pound cake.

Whip the cream with the confectioners' sugar. Take half of the whipped cream mixture and fold in the raspberries, ⅓ cup Grand Marnier and the toasted almonds. Into the other half of the whipped cream mixture fold the semisweet chocolate.

Brush the cake lining the bowl with some of the brandy. Pour raspberry whipped cream into the bowl. Cover with more slices of pound cake. Brush that layer of pound cake with the 3 tablespoons Grand Marnier. Pour in chocolate whipped cream, cover with pound cake, brush on remainder of brandy. Cover with plastic wrap, put into refrigerator for 6 hours, or overnight. Next day, unmold onto serving platter and slice into wedges.

Serves 12–16.

Lizzie O'Rourke

THE FIVE CROWNS RESTAURANT, located in California, is a duplicate of the oldest inn in England. So who better than the restaurant's Chef **Ivan Harrison** to give us a classic recipe for English Trifle?

English Trifle

1 4½-ounce package vanilla pudding and pie filling mix
2 cups light cream
2 tablespoons dark Puerto Rican rum
2¼ cups heavy cream
3 tablespoons granulated sugar
2 tablespoons red raspberry preserves
1 10-inch diameter round sponge cake
¼ cup brandy
¼ cup dry sherry
30 whole strawberries

Combine pudding mix and light cream. Cook, stirring constantly, until mixture comes to a boil and thickens. Add rum; chill. Whip 1¼ cups heavy cream and 1 tablespoon sugar until stiff. Fold into chilled pudding. Take a deep bowl, 10 inches in diameter, and coat the inside with raspberry preserves to within 1 inch of the top. Slice cake horizontally into fourths. Place top slice, crust side up, in bottom of bowl, curving edges of cake upward. Combine brandy and sherry; sprinkle a quarter of the mixture (about 2 tablespoons) over the cake slice. Repeat procedure twice. Arrange half of strawberries on top layer of pudding. Cover with remaining cake layer, crust side down. Sprinkle with remaining brandy-sherry mixture. Whip remaining 1 cup cream and 2 tablespoons sugar until stiff. Place whipped cream in pastry bag with fluted tip. Make 12 mounds around edge of bowl and 3 mounds across diameter. Top each mound with a strawberry. Chill at least 6 hours. To serve, spoon onto chilled dessert plates.

Serves 12.

CHEF IVAN HARRISON

Printed by permission of Five Crowns Restaurant.

CHOCOLATE crêpes, dark chocolate sauce and whipped cream. Need I say more? **Joan Steur** presented this "chocolate fettuccine," a recipe of chef Martin Johner and food writer Gary A. Goldberg, one day, and the staff and crew are *still* talking about it!

Fettuccine alla Panna

Chocolate Crêpes

>   3 large eggs
> ⅔ cup half-and-half or light cream
>   2 tablespoons granulated sugar
> ⅔ cup water
> ⅛ teaspoon salt
>   3 tablespoons clarified butter, melted and cooled, plus a
>   small amount to grease crêpe pan
>   1 cup less 1 tablespoon Wondra flour
>   2 tablespoons unsweetened cocoa

Dark Chocolate Sauce

>   5 ounces semisweet chocolate, coarsely chopped
>   1 ounce unsweetened baking chocolate, coarsely chopped
> ¼ cup granulated sugar
> ½ cup hot brewed espresso coffee
>   2 tablespoons almond-flavored liqueur (Amaretto)
>   2 tablespoons butter

Whipped Cream

>   1 cup heavy cream, well chilled
>   1 tablespoon confectioners' sugar
>   1 teaspoon vanilla

Combine all ingredients for crêpes in bowl of food processor or blender and process until smooth. Pour batter through fine-mesh strainer into measuring cup and let rest for 20 minutes.

Grease a 6-inch diameter crêpe pan with a small amount of clarified butter. Heat pan over medium-high heat, until drop of water sizzles upon contact. Pour ¼ cup of batter into pan, swirl quickly to cover pan bottom with batter. Immediately pour excess batter back into measuring cup, and cook crêpe on one side until edges brown lightly. Flip and cook for 15–20 seconds. Repeat until all batter is used. Let crêpes cool.

Using a very sharp knife, cut each crêpe into long, thin strands about ⅜ inch in width. Separate so that strands resemble fettuccine.

To prepare sauce, melt all chocolate in top of double boiler over hot, not boiling, water. Dissolve sugar in hot coffee and add to melted chocolate. Mix well. Add almond-flavored liqueur and butter. Blend well. Remove sauce from heat. Cool. Reheat before serving.

Combine heavy cream, confectioners' sugar and vanilla. Whip until soft peaks are formed.

To serve, place chocolate "fettuccine" in a large shallow serving bowl. Gently form a well in the center and spoon whipped cream into the well. Toss "fettuccine" with whipped cream. Serve in individual bowls. Drizzle warm chocolate sauce over each portion. Additional chocolate sauce may be passed.

Tips

Storing Crêpes. There is no need to put waxed paper between crêpes unless planning to freeze them. Crêpes are most tender if not refrigerated; but they can be made a day or two ahead, tightly sealed in foil and stored, then brought back to room temperature in a steamer or microwave oven.

Chocolate Sauce. I prefer a dark bittersweet sauce, so I mix coarsely chopped semisweet and unsweetened chocolate and add strong espresso coffee. The sauce should be served warm, not piping hot. As it cools, it thickens slightly and coats the "pasta" (sliced crêpes) more evenly. The sauce can be made several days ahead, stored in a covered container in refrigerator and reheated for use.

Whipped Cream. Do not overwhip cream in this recipe; it should be whipped only until soft peaks form. I whip the cream by hand, using a chilled whisk and a stainless steel bowl set into a larger bowl filled with ice cubes. The cream can be whipped several hours ahead, covered and stored in the refrigerator.

Makes 14–16 6-inch crêpes; 1½ cups sauce.

JOAN STEUR

I S there anybody who isn't a chocolate lover? **Ellen Katzman** visited *Hour*'s kitchen and created mouth-watering, scrumptious chocolate candies that'll make a chocoholic out of you after you've tasted them. You can also dip your favorite fruit in chocolate; Ellen says that you can buy dry or glazed fruits at a health food store. If you want to use fresh fruits, try grapes, bananas, kiwis, oranges or strawberries. (Note: Do not dip fresh pineapple.)

Chocolate Candies

How to temper chocolate: First determine if the product you are using is *real* chocolate or an imitation. If it is *real* chocolate, it will contain cocoa butter.

To temper real chocolate, melt three-quarters of your total volume in a double boiler at a very low heat. Using a food processor or vegetable grater, grate the balance of your chocolate into a very coarse powder. Blend the grated chocolate into the melted chocolate. Using either your hand or a spoon, stir chocolate until it feels cold to the touch (about 20 minutes for 2 pounds). If you have tempered your chocolate properly, it will begin to set within 10 minutes of this final step, if not, remelt and try again.

Proper melting temperatures: Heat to 100°, cool to 85°, reheat to 91°.

It is best to let your chocolate-dipped fruits set at room temperature (if it is below 72°), or in the refrigerator. *Never* put chocolate-dipped fruits in the freezer to set.

ELLEN KATZMAN

Charo offers her Quesadilla to the audience; unfortunately there weren't enough to go around. (Page 100.)

For once, I get a chance to hand down a verdict on Judge (Joseph) Wapner. (Page 102.)

"Operator, could you please reverse the charges?" (Pat Sajak, page 105.)

Back . . . back . . . don't worry, there's enough for everybody! (Gloria Loring, page 112.)

I don't know, Dinah, it gives me a warm feeling here, but will it go away? (Dinah Shore, page 110.)

Rule #1: Never pick up a pot without a pot holder! (Ann Jillian, page 114.)

Geoffrey Holder insisted that I get into costume to fully appreciate his Caribbean cooking! (Page 115.)

Vincent Price said that the only way to really enjoy his Potted Shrimp was to be a little potted—so we sampled his special Bloody Marys. (Page 117.)

Chances are, you'll find this dish wonderful, wonderful—but—it's not for me to say. (Johnny Mathis, page 118.)

Nancy, are you sure the lobster's dead? (Nancy Walker, page 120.)

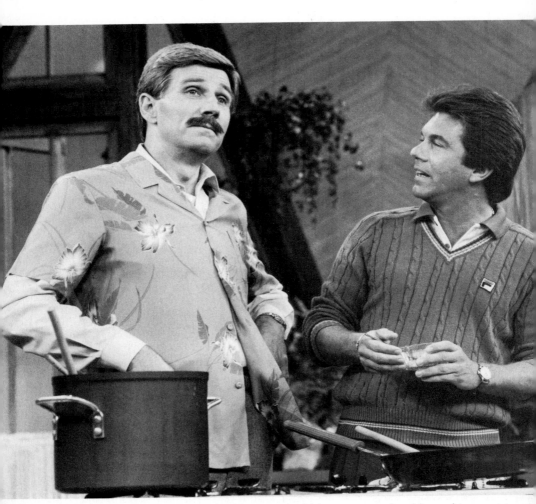

I thought Larry Manetti, from *Magnum P.I.,* would be more comfortable cooking next to a familiar face. (Page 119.)

If I eat it all up, will I get something under my pillow? (Dody Goodman, page 120.)

I like my food sharp, but this could get dangerous! (Maxene Andrews, page 121.)

Toni, will you stop singing and cook! (Toni Tennille, page 123.)

Victoria, if this food's the reason you look so good, I'm eating it every day!
(Victoria Principal, page 125.)

A Gracious First Lady offers some homemade treats to the *Hour* crew. (Page 127.)

When Mickey Gilley said we're doing some down-home cooking, he was serious. He brought his mom! (Mickey Gilley and mom, Irene, page 128.)

Chocolate Roll—yes, yes, Nanette. (Nanette Fabray, page 131.)

But first, a spot of tea. (Lynn Redgrave, page 129.)

Jane Fonda and Mignon McCarthy, co-author of *Women Coming of Age,* make an energy drink for me. (Page 133.)

It's very important to remember, when you try making pizza in your kitchen: Move the boom microphone out of the way *before* twirling the pizza. (Page 26.)

Mother Wonderful—obviously talking about something that's close to her heart. (Myra Chanin, page 137.)

Laurie and I have sampled many of the dishes she's made on the air, and one thing we can tell you—there is no graceful way to eat on camera! (Laurie Burrows Grad, page 139.)

"Try it Gary, you'll like it." Bert Greene swore to me that I would! (Page 143.)

Margo Kidushim's Moussaka—waiting for the moment of truth! (Page 144.)

Jackie, are you *sure* you measured that right? (Jackie Olden, page 146.)

A master shows me the way—to drop it all over the counter! (Chef Tell, page 148.)

You would normally have to watch *Hour Magazine* all week to see these experts, but on this night they all came together to celebrate our show's anniversary!

From left to right—psychiatrist Dr. William Rader, columnist Abigail Van Buren (Dear Abby), Gary, pediatrician Dr. Loraine Stern, cardiologist Dr. Isadore Rosenfeld, hairstylist to the stars José Eber.

Does this *really* work? (Heloise, page 170.)

Backstage—where all the magic begins! *From left to right*—Chris Circosta, prop master; Marty Berman, executive producer; Gary; Steve Clements, producer; and Glen Swanson, director.

2

CELEBRITIES

When I think back about some of the celebrity cooking spots, I guess I would have to say that they were among my favorite segments on the show. Cooking with people often leads to insights about them that are rarely revealed in a typical celebrity sit-down interview.

As I went over the list of guests who cooked with me, memories of their visits came to mind . . .

I knew when I invited the outrageous **Rip Taylor** into the *Hour Magazine* kitchen that laughter and hysteria would be a part of the recipe. When he presented Rip's Roll-ups, the simplicity of the ingredients and preparation didn't really come across as simple—I'd say that had everything to do with his inimitable style. I imagine the recipe won't be as difficult (or hilarious) for you to follow, but it will provide a tasty and nutritious appetizer!

Rip's Roll-ups

12 asparagus tips, steamed
12 slices Swiss cheese
12 slices ham
    Hollandaise sauce

Put an asparagus tip and a slice of Swiss cheese on top of a ham slice and roll it up. Place in pan, seam side down. Top with Hollandaise sauce. Repeat until all ingredients are used. Cook in microwave oven a couple of minutes (until cheese in center melts). Cut into bite-size pieces and insert a toothpick in each. Place on serving tray and serve as hors d'oeuvres.

Tips

Use paper plates—no mess. Microwave cooking will keep cheese from getting stringy.

Makes about 36.

RIP TAYLOR

EVERYBODY knows **Charo** is vivacious, explosive, unpredictable and sexy, but few realize that behind that "cuchi-cuchi" exterior lies a serious musician and a woman devoted to her family. You can see that she really enjoys cooking and entertaining. She offered us a delicious, simple, easy-to-make dish that can be served as an hors d'oeuvre to start off any meal, or as a late-night snack.

Quesadilla

Corn tortilla
Chicken or turkey leftovers, cut up
Grated American cheese

On a corn tortilla, place some chicken or turkey and cover with cheese. Cook over low heat in a slightly greased pan until cheese melts.

Makes 1.

CHARO

THE sushi craze has hit America, but how many of us know how to make it ourselves? **Katherine Helmond,** whom we remember as Jessica Tate on *Soap,* can now be seen on *Who's the Boss?* She presented a recipe that's simple and unusual at the same time! Don't let the Japanese name *kappamaki* intimidate you.

Kappamaki (Sushi)

Filling

> 2 cups cold water
> 1 cup uncooked brown rice
> ½ cup wheat berries
> ½ teaspoon sea salt, or 1 teaspoon tamari (soy sauce)
>   Scallions, or cucumber and/or chives, if desired—experiment!
>   Japanese green mustard

Wrapping

> Nori seaweed sheets

Heat water to a boil. Add rice, wheat berries and salt or tamari. Lower heat to simmer. Cover pan and let mixture steam for 45–50 minutes, or until water is absorbed.

Lay seaweed out on a bamboo sushi roller. Spread a row of rice on one end. Lay scallions, which have been sliced lengthwise, on rice. Spread mustard on scallions. Use sparingly—it's quite hot! Roll up into a long, rice-filled seaweed roll. To seal, dampen the loose edge of the seaweed with water, soy sauce or beer. Slice roll in 1-inch lengths and serve.

Note

Tamari soy sauce, brown rice, wheat berries and nori seaweed sheets may be purchased at any natural-foods store. Japanese green mustard may be found in the Oriental foods section of your supermarket, or in an Oriental grocery, as may the soy sauce.

Makes 40–48.

KATHERINE HELMOND

Eggplant Hors d'Oeuvres

    1 eggplant
    ¼ onion
    1 clove garlic
    1 jar Cara Mia artichokes
    2 celery ribs
    ⅓ small jar capers
    1 tomato
   12 cocktail onions
   12 green olives with pimiento centers
    1 jar sliced mushrooms, *or* 6 large mushrooms, sliced
      Juice of 1 lemon
    4 tablespoons wine vinegar
    2 tablespoons olive oil
    6 pinches oregano
      Salt and pepper to taste

Bake eggplant 1 hour at 350°. Peel, chop in food processor. Dice onion, mash garlic, cut up artichokes, reserving juice. Dice celery, mince tomato, cut cocktail onions and olives in half. Add all the above ingredients and the mushrooms to the eggplant, processing briefly between additions. Add lemon juice and wine vinegar, olive oil, oregano, salt and pepper to taste. Blend thoroughly, chill for 6–24 hours. Serve with crackers.

Serves 10.

JUDGE JOSEPH A. WAPNER

ONE of the most memorable and unique cooking demonstrations was by **Jo Anne Worley,** of *Laugh-In* fame, who gave us beauty tips while making breakfast! Who else would use the flour and oil in the kitchen on her face as a makeup base? And Jo Anne was the only guest in the history of *Hour Magazine* who got an omelet to sing "Mammy." Try it!

Fluffy, Puffy Omelet

6 eggs, separated
6 tablespoons water
1 teaspoon salt
　Dash pepper
2 tablespoons fat or salad oil

Heat oven to 325°. In large bowl of electric mixer, beat egg whites with water and salt until stiff. Beat egg yolks and pepper in different bowl. Then fold yolks into egg whites. Add salad oil to a hot 10-inch skillet—one that can go in oven—tipping pan to cover bottom with oil. Pour omelet mixture into hot skillet and cook over low heat about 5 minutes, or until fluffy and puffy. Bake in same pan for 12–15 minutes.

To serve omelet, loosen edges with spatula, and either tear it into wedges like a pie, or cut down center (not all the way) and fold in half. Serve on hot dish.

Serves 3–6.

JO ANNE WORLEY

CREOLE food is certainly making it big across America. This roast beef recipe was presented by the talented **Linda Hopkins,** and I remember the importance of adding just the right amount of cayenne. It probably helps her hit those incredible high notes!

Creole Roast Beef

3–4 pounds roast beef
2 tablespoons garlic salt
2 tablespoons onion salt
2½ tablespoons Adolph's Meat Tenderizer
½ teaspoon cayenne pepper
1 teaspoon black pepper
6 bay leaves
4 onions
4 cloves of garlic
1 medium bell pepper
1 generous tablespoon Crisco oil
1 stick butter (½ cup)
1 tablespoon oregano, or to taste
1 package mushroom gravy mix
Salt to taste

Season meat with garlic salt, onion salt, meat tenderizer, cayenne pepper and black pepper. Set meat on aluminum foil and top with 2 bay leaves on each side (4 total). Now wrap foil around meat and put in freezer overnight.

Preheat oven to 350°. Put frozen meat, still wrapped in foil, in oven and cook for 45 minutes. While meat is cooking, cut up the onions, garlic and bell pepper, and sauté in Crisco and butter. Add remaining 2 bay leaves and oregano, and sauté together. Separately, make mushroom gravy as directed on package. Add to sautéed mixture and stir well.

Take meat out and open foil. Pour gravy over meat, rewrap and put back in oven; turn up to 400°. Cook for 30 minutes. Serve.

Serves 6–10.

LINDA HOPKINS

THE versatile **Pat Sajak** is currently hosting the most successful syndicated show in history, *Wheel of Fortune*. When he visited *Hour Magazine* to present his Ground-Nut Stew, he had to stop in the middle and call his wife to check on the correct ingredients. We're certainly glad she was at home to save the stew.

Ground-Nut Stew

Condiments

Chopped tomatoes; chopped green pepper; sliced bananas, sprinkled with lemon juice; coconut; chopped onions; chunky pineapple; chopped oranges; salted peanuts.

1½ cups uncooked rice
3 cups water
¼ cup oil or butter
½ cup peanut butter, crunchy or otherwise
¼ cup all-purpose flour
Chicken broth, reserved from stewing chicken
Half-and-half
4 hard-boiled eggs, peeled and diced
4 potatoes, boiled in their jackets, peeled and diced
1 4–5 pound chicken, stewed, meat taken from bones, reserve liquid

Prepare as much of each condiment as necessary to allow each person 2 tablespoons of each. Set rice to cook. While rice is cooking, make gravy. Heat oil and peanut butter in skillet, stir in flour and add as much chicken broth and half-and-half as necessary. Add eggs, potatoes and chicken to the gravy.

To serve, place a bed of rice on each plate. Top with the chicken-gravy mixture. Add 2 tablespoons each of the condiments. *Do not omit anything,* even if your guests tell you they don't like green pepper. They will.

Tip

Great for a party. Guests can supply condiments.

Serves 6–8.

PAT SAJAK

Texas Chili

2 pounds lean ground round
1 small can Ortega chilies
1 green pepper, chopped
1–2 tomatoes, chopped
2 cups tomato sauce
1 onion, chopped
1–2 celery stalks, chopped
1 red pepper, chopped

Brown and drain meat. Cut chilies down middle, remove seeds, slice and add with remaining ingredients. Simmer 30–60 minutes.

Note

The amounts of the ingredients can be changed according to your personal taste.

Serves 3–4.

JENILEE HARRISON

"Capital Punishment" Chili

4 pounds extra-lean chuck, flank or round steak, coarsely ground (chili ground)

1 pound extra-lean chuck, flank or round steak, cut into
   ¼-inch cubes
2 pounds extra-lean pork loin, cut into ¼-inch cubes
2 large onions, finely chopped
8–10 cloves garlic, finely chopped
2 tablespoons paprika
1 teaspoon mole powder
1–2 tablespoons flaked or ground chili peppers, to taste
1 6-ounce can tomato paste
2 10½-ounce cans beef bouillon or broth
4 tablespoons ground cumin
1 tablespoon ground oregano
2 tablespoons MSG
2 12-ounce cans/bottles beer
1 tablespoon masa harina or cornmeal
   Hot water

Brown meat in large skillet until fat is cooked off. Transfer meat to an 8-quart stockpot. Sauté onions and garlic in pan drippings until tender, then add meat and mix well. Add remaining ingredients, except masa harina and hot water, and mix well. Simmer for 2 hours. Mix masa harina with enough hot water to make a light paste and add to chili 30 minutes before serving, to thicken.

Note

Amounts of spices and chili pepper may be changed to suit individual preference.

Serves 12.

PRESENTED BY PETER MARSHALL

CARMEN Zapata, who's been seen on so many TV shows and on her own series, called *Viva Valdez*, brought a little Mexican flavor into our kitchen. Appropriately so! She suggests serving her Albóndigas in Chili Chipolte as a main course, with Mexican rice, flour tortillas and cold beer.

Albóndigas in Chili Chipolte
(Meatballs in Chili Sauce)

1 large can peeled tomatoes
1 7-ounce can chipolte chilies
2 cloves garlic
  Salt and pepper
½ pound lean ground beef
½ pound lean ground pork
1 raw egg
⅛ cup bread crumbs
1 hard-boiled egg, chopped

In a blender, put ¾ can of peeled tomatoes with its juice. Add 2 chilies *only*, and a little sauce from the chili can; 1 clove garlic, chopped fine; and salt and pepper to taste. Liquefy. Set aside. In a separate bowl, mix ground beef and pork. Add raw egg to mixture, along with 1 clove garlic, chopped fine; add bread crumbs and salt and pepper to taste. Mix well.

Put tomato mixture in a pot and bring to a boil. In the meantime, make about 8 small meat patties. Add just a little chopped hard-boiled egg in center of each patty, and form meat around it to make a meatball. When tomato mixture comes to a boil, add meatballs, cover pot and simmer for about 1 hour and 15 minutes. If sauce becomes too thick, add a little water.

Serves 2–3.

CARMEN ZAPATA

DELLA **Reese**'s songs won't actually make you get up and cha-cha, but her chicken recipe might. It's soulful, just like its presenter, and it will get your tastebuds dancing too!

Cha-Cha Chicken Wings

18 chicken wings, about 3 pounds
   Cayenne pepper
   Paprika
2 tablespoons bacon fat
2 10¾-ounce cans Campbell's condensed tomato soup
½ cup water
1 large onion, chopped
2 medium green peppers, chopped
3 cups hot cooked rice

Sprinkle chicken generously with cayenne pepper and paprika. In 10-inch skillet over medium heat, in hot bacon fat, cook chicken wings until brown on all sides. Stir in soup, water and onion. Reduce heat to low; cover. Simmer 15 minutes, stirring occasionally. Uncover; add green pepper. Simmer 15 minutes more, or until chicken is fork tender, stirring occasionally. Serve with cooked rice.

Serves 6.

PRESENTED BY DELLA REESE

Printed by permission of Campbell Soup Company.

THE multi-talented **Dinah Shore** established her cooking expertise years ago. Needless to say, she felt at home in the *Hour Magazine* kitchen, and I was glad to be in the kitchen with Dinah—who could resist? She presented Kleeman's Chicken on Corn Bread—Kleeman's was the name of a famous restaurant in Nashville, Tennessee. The restaurant is now closed, but the recipe will live on.

Kleeman's Chicken on Corn Bread

Chicken

8 chicken breasts
Water
Salt and pepper to taste
Grated ginger to taste
2 stalks celery, with tops
1 large carrot
4 sprigs parsley
1 whole onion

Corn Bread

1 cup cornmeal
1 cup all-purpose flour
½ teaspoon baking soda
1 teaspoon baking powder
1 teaspoon salt
6 tablespoons shortening
1 cup buttermilk
2 eggs

Sauce

6 tablespoons minced onion
1 cup butter
8 tablespoons all-purpose flour
3 pints chicken broth
½ cup cream or milk
Salt and pepper to taste

Place the chicken breasts in water to cover. Add salt, pepper, grated ginger, celery, carrot, parsley and onion. Cook until just done. Keep warm. Use the strained broth for your sauce.

Preheat oven to 400°. Sift dry ingredients for corn bread into a mixing bowl. Cut in shortening until well blended. In a separate bowl, beat buttermilk and eggs together. Mix with dry ingredients until just blended. Pour into a well-greased oblong baking dish. Bake for 25 minutes, or until done. Corn bread should be just baked and very hot when served. It's best that way.

While corn bread bakes, make sauce. Brown minced onion in butter until golden. Add flour. Add chicken broth, cream or milk, salt and pepper. Cook to desired thickness. Keep warm.

Slice chicken, place on split corn bread and pour sauce over top. Serve extra sauce on the side. You'll need it—it's that good! Be prepared to serve seconds on this one.

Serves 10–12.

DINAH SHORE

Reprinted by permission of Doubleday & Co., Inc., from *Someone's in the Kitchen with Dinah* by Dinah Shore. Copyright © 1971 by Dinah Shore.

WEALTHY and willful is the way **Liz Curtis** goes through each crisis on *Days of Our Lives*—not exactly the kind of woman you'd expect to see with her apron on in the kitchen! But that's where Liz ends and Gloria Loring begins. She prepared an easy-to-make Chicken Piccata for us when she visited *Hour*'s kitchen.

Chicken Piccata

4 chicken breasts, boned and skinned
Salt
Pepper
Juice of 1 lemon
2 tablespoons unsalted butter
½ cup dry white wine
1 tablespoon capers

Flatten chicken to a scallopini thickness, using a tenderizer, hammer or the edge of a plate. Salt and pepper and sprinkle with lemon juice. Allow to marinate for about 2 hours.

Heat butter in a frying pan and add breasts. Sauté approximately 5 minutes on each side. Remove to hot platter to keep warm. Deglaze the pan with wine. Add capers and pour over chicken.

Serves 4.

GLORIA LORING

I NDIAN cooking and heartburn always went hand in hand for me. But thanks to actress and former Miss India **Persis Khambatta,** this savory entrée for two actually changed my mind!

Rogan Josh (Indian Curry)

Shortening
1 large onion, finely chopped
2 whole cloves
2 cardamom seeds
¾-inch piece whole ginger root and ¼ clove garlic, both finely minced, mashed together with 1 teaspoon water to make paste
¼ teaspoon cumin powder
¼ teaspoon turmeric
¼ teaspoon paprika
¼ teaspoon red chili powder
1 large can peeled tomatoes
1 pound lean lamb (or chicken without skin)

In a skillet, in a little shortening, brown onion slightly. Add cloves and cardamom seeds, and fry over medium heat. Stir in ½ teaspoon of ginger-garlic paste (save rest in refrigerator for future use).

In curries, you blend the spices well; that's the secret. Mix together the cumin powder, turmeric, paprika and red chili powder, add to onion mixture and stir well. Add tomatoes and a little juice from the can, and stir to make a thick gravy—keep stirring to prevent burning. Add raw meat and stir well. Cover pan and lower heat slightly. Cook until meat is done. Add water or tomato juice if it gets dry. Serve with rice or pilau.

Serves 2.

PERSIS KHAMBATTA

THIS next recipe sounds fancy, but it deserves a place in your collection. Cooking a goose just the right way takes some skill and finesse. Actress **Ann Jillian** of *It's a Living* brought us this recipe—along with some Lithuanian traditions.

Lithuanian Roast Goose and Sauerkraut

8–10 pound goose
4 pounds sauerkraut—preferably champagne cured
2 cups chopped onion
2 cups chopped apples—preferably tart ones
½ teaspoon salt
1 tablespoon granulated sugar
1 tablespoon caraway seeds
1 large carrot, shredded
1 teaspoon freshly ground pepper
1 teaspoon salt
½ teaspoon ground allspice

Preheat oven to 325°. Pull out all loose fat from inside goose. Dice fat and render in small saucepan. Drain sauerkraut, wash well under running water and squeeze dry. Heat ½ cup of rendered goose fat in heavy 10-inch or 12-inch skillet. Add chopped onion, sauté until transparent. Add squeezed kraut, sauté until golden. Cover and simmer for 10 minutes. Transfer kraut and onion mixture into large mixing bowl. Add chopped apple, ½ teaspoon salt, the sugar, caraway seeds, shredded carrot and a few grindings of pepper. Mix.

Wash goose inside and out. Dry with paper towels and sprinkle cavity with 1 teaspoon salt and the allspice. Fill goose with stuffing. Sew up openings with needle and thread, or use skewers. Truss legs with cord. Tie wings to body with cord. Set goose breast up on a rack in a large roasting pan. Cook in middle of oven for 2½–3 hours, or 20–25 minutes per pound. Use a baster to remove grease that drips into pan. For last ½ hour, raise oven temperature to 350°. Puncture goose skin with fork to let grease out. Remove to platter and allow to rest 10–15 minutes before carving.

Serves 6.

ANN JILLIAN

SOMEONE once described **Geoffrey Holder** as a one-man cultural center. Why? Because he's a superb dancer, actor, singer, artist, photographer, author, poet and choreographer—and, believe it or not, a sensational gourmet cook. By the time he was through with his Sautéed Red Snapper it looked more like a culinary work of art than an edible entrée. You can't go wrong with this one!

Sautéed Red Snapper

2 cloves garlic, minced
2 tablespoons olive oil
2 tablespoons butter
2 pounds red snapper filets
2 tomatoes, chopped
2 scallions, both green and white parts
2 ounces cognac
2 tablespoons grated Parmesan cheese
Tabasco to taste

Sauté garlic in oil and butter. Add fish. Top with tomatoes and scallions, and simmer for 3–4 minutes. Turn over and simmer for additional 3–4 minutes. Add cognac, cheese and Tabasco; cook for 3 more minutes. Serve with rice.

Serves 4–6.

GEOFFREY HOLDER

ACTRESS **Celia Weston** certainly fit in in our *Hour Magazine* kitchen. Obviously, hanging around Mel's Diner every week on the TV hit series *Alice* taught her something about cooking, even though her Carolina Shrimp Royale never quite made the menu at Mel's!

Carolina Shrimp Royale

1–2 pounds large shrimp
1 cup vinegar
1 cup chopped onion
⅔ cup chopped celery
2 tablespoons bacon grease or drippings
1 tablespoon all-purpose flour
1 teaspoon salt
2 tablespoons fresh basil
¼ cup chili powder, or to taste
1 cup water
2 cups diced tomatoes
1 can small English peas
1 tablespoon granulated sugar
⅓ to ½ cup sherry
Hot cooked rice

Wash shrimp. Place in large saucepan with 1 cup vinegar and enough boiling water to cover. Bring to a boil, cover pan and simmer until shrimp are tender (shells turn pink), about 8–12 minutes. Cool and drain. Peel and devein shrimp.

In skillet, brown onion and celery in bacon grease. Add flour, salt, basil and chili powder. Slowly add water and cook for 15 minutes. Add tomatoes, peas and sugar, and cook 10 minutes more before adding shrimp and sherry. Warm shrimp thoroughly. Serve over rice.

Serves 4–8.

CELIA WESTON

IT'S hard to think seriously of following the recipe of a man who's known as Dr. Death, and who once buried his sister alive in a movie called *The Fall of the House of Usher*. But, despite the tendencies of the characters he plays, veteran actor **Vincent Price** is truly a gourmet chef and has two cookbooks to his credit. I must admit, lightning *did* strike as we opened our kitchen doors to him, but Potted Shrimp was a real "thriller" to eat!

Potted Shrimp

1 stick (½ cup) butter
¼ teaspoon mace
¼ teaspoon nutmeg
½ teaspoon salt
2 cups cooked, peeled and deveined shrimp

Melt the butter. Heat until it is hot, but not bubbling. Add to the melted butter the mace, nutmeg and salt. Have the shrimp ready. They should be whole, but not too big. Pour a little of the melted butter over the shrimp, making certain that each shrimp is well coated with the butter. Put shrimp into a large mold or 6 small individual crocks, and press down, taking care not to crush the shrimp. Pour the remaining melted butter on top and chill in the refrigerator until firm. Potted shrimp will keep, well refrigerated, for about a week.

Serve in the individual crocks, or turned out of a larger mold onto a bed of shredded lettuce, accompanied by slices of thin brown bread, melba toast or crackers.

Serves 6.

VINCENT PRICE

J OHNNY Mathis, whose record sales are in excess of one hundred million albums, has performed for presidents, heads of state, royal families and concertgoers in every country of the world. But besides earning the title as the most romantic singer of all time, he also excels as a gourmet cook. His book, *Cooking for You Alone,* includes Johnny's recipe for Shrimp Scampi. When he cooked it for us, it was every bit as wonderful as his love songs.

Shrimp Scampi

2 tablespoons butter
1 clove garlic, minced
4 jumbo shrimp, peeled and deveined (tails left on)
1 teaspoon lemon juice
1 tablespoon grated Parmesan cheese
   Salt and pepper
¼ teaspoon parsley flakes

Melt butter in 10-inch skillet over medium heat. Stir in garlic and sauté briefly. Add shrimp and sauté 1–2 minutes on each side. Pour lemon juice over shrimp. Add cheese. Salt and pepper to taste. Sauté briefly. Remove shrimp to serving plate and keep warm. Raise heat under skillet and boil pan juices until syrupy. Stir in parsley. Pour sauce over shrimp.

Served over rice this is an outstanding entrée, or it can be used alone as a premeal or cocktail party appetizer.

Serves 1–2.

JOHNNY MATHIS

TOM Selleck would be willing to give up his papaya for this pasta says his co-star on *Magnum P.I.*, Larry Manetti. It *was* delicious—so simple, so good—really one of the best ever on *Hour Magazine*.

Linguine and Clam Sauce

1 pound linguine
⅓ cup olive oil
½ stick (¼ cup) butter
3 cloves garlic, pressed or minced
4 6½-ounce cans minced clams, including liquid
1 teaspoon dried oregano
¼ teaspoon pepper, or to taste
2 tablespoons chopped fresh parsley
  Grated Romano cheese

In large pot of boiling water, cook linguine just until tender. Meanwhile, in small saucepan, heat oil and butter until butter melts. Add garlic, cook until golden. Stir in clams with their liquid, oregano, pepper and parsley. Cook until heated, about 5 minutes. Drain linguine, return to pot. Add clam sauce. Toss and serve with grated Romano cheese and Italian Toast (see below).

Italian Toast

Put a little olive oil on a split loaf, or 1 piece of bread for each person. Mix chopped tomatoes, onion and a little fresh basil, and put it on bread. Toast lightly. And that's it.

Serves 4.

LARRY MANETTI

ACTRESS, comedienne and director **Nancy Walker** prepared one of my all-time favorites—Lobster with Linguine. I wonder if she ever cooked for Rhoda as well as she did for us? Nancy was energetic and hilarious, as usual, and her lobster was outstanding!

Lobster with Linguine

½ cup oil
Chopped garlic to taste
Dried red pepper to taste
Mint to taste
2 large cans chopped tomatoes
1 lobster, cooked and quartered
Hot cooked linguine

Put oil in a large pot over medium heat. Add garlic and cook for 5 minutes, stirring constantly so it won't burn. Add red pepper, stir for 5 minutes; add mint and stir for 5 minutes more. Add tomatoes and simmer for 15 minutes. Now add the quartered lobster. Cook for 10 minutes. Serve lobster on top of linguine.

Serves 2–4.

NANCY WALKER

"FAIRY Pudding"—whose else would prepare a tuna casserole and give it a name like that? **Dody Goodman** as chef—one more role she can fill with success—told me that when she was a young dancer in New York City, and short on funds, she and the other gals would make this inexpensive dish.

Fairy Pudding (Tuna Casserole)

1 7-ounce can tuna fish
1 can mushroom soup
2½ cups hot cooked rice
Potato chips

Preheat oven to 350°. Mix tuna and soup in casserole dish, and heat in oven until hot. Serve over rice; top with potato chips.

Serves 2–3.

DODY GOODMAN

LONG before the Supremes and the Beatles, there were three singing sisters named Andrews. Together they made musical history. So what can you say about a living legend? **Maxene Andrews** visited us and "boogie-woogied" her way to a Greek-style rice pilaf.

Rice Pilaf Greek Style

¼ cup pine nuts
½ cup tiny egg noodles
1 cup rice
1 tablespoon Fleischmann's Light margarine
2½ cups chicken stock (homemade is best)

Heat large saucepan over medium heat. Add pine nuts and noodles, crushing noodles in your hand as you add them. Stir constantly until pine nuts and noodles begin to brown. Add rice and stir for about 1 minute. Add margarine, stir until melted. Then slowly and carefully add chicken stock. Cover and simmer for 20–25 minutes, or until all water has been absorbed.
Serve with chicken.

Serves 4–6.

MAXENE ANDREWS

Sautéed Vegetable Melt

1 tablespoon sesame oil
1 medium onion, minced
2 cloves garlic, chopped
2 cups diced zucchini
2 cups diced pattypan squash
1 cup diced yellow summer squash
½ teaspoon dill weed
½ teaspoon salt
1 cup diced eggplant
1 cup sliced mushrooms
2 cups shredded Cheddar cheese

Preheat broiler. Heat sesame oil in a large heavy skillet. Add onion and garlic, and sauté until tender. Add zucchini, pattypan, summer squash, dill weed and salt. Reduce heat, cover, and cook 5 minutes. Add eggplant and mushrooms. Cover and cook 10 minutes longer. Transfer mixture to 4 individual baking dishes. Top each with ½ cup cheese. Place under broiler until cheese bubbles. Serve vegetable melt with brown rice, and melon or strawberries for dessert.

Serves 4.

BYRON ALLEN

RUTH **Buzzi** is one of television's funniest comediennes. She brought a recipe for Savoy Cabbage—and I remember it as one of the funniest cooking spots ever! Her outrageous and zany personality came out in preparing this healthful vegetable dish—*Laugh-In* continued on *Hour Magazine*.

Savoy Cabbage

1 tablespoon oil
1 head of Savoy cabbage, cut into medium-size pieces
2 pickled banana peppers, medium to large
½ 8-ounce can Hunt's tomato sauce
   Water, ¼ cup or less
   Salt and pepper to taste

Heat oil in saucepan. Add cabbage and stir thoroughly. Cut tops off banana peppers and pour any juice out of peppers onto cabbage. Cut up peppers into small pieces, adding to cabbage in saucepan. Add tomato sauce. Stir well. Add the water and salt and pepper. Cook over low heat for 1½ hours, covered. The cabbage should look totally soft and "weak."
   Best when refrigerated and reheated before eating.

Serves 4–6.

RUTH BUZZI

A great singer and a great cook, **Toni Tennille** visited us and prepared her Vegetarian Rice Creole. She claims it's the way to her Captain's heart. And she added that, for a perfect vegetarian meal, you should serve it with a steamed green vegetable, such as broccoli.

Vegetarian Rice Creole

2 onions (purple squash), chopped
   Olive oil
3 bell peppers, chopped
3–4 stalks celery, chopped
2–3 fresh Italian pear-shaped tomatoes, chopped (3 cups)

1 cup brown rice, washed
2 8-ounce cans tomato sauce
  Juice of ½ lemon
2 tablespoons sweet basil
  Cayenne pepper to taste
  Spike or seasoning salt to taste
  Sharp Cheddar cheese, grated

Sauté onion in olive oil until golden. Add bell peppers and celery, and simmer until tender crisp. Add chopped tomatoes. Cover and simmer until tomatoes cook down and become liquefied. Add brown rice along with the tomato sauce, lemon juice and sweet basil. Add cayenne pepper and Spike or seasoning salt. Bring to a boil, then lower heat and simmer 50 minutes. Preheat broiler.

Place rice in a casserole dish. Sprinkle generously with grated sharp Cheddar cheese. Place under broiler until cheese is bubbly and golden.

Serves 3–6.

TONI TENNILLE

WE'VE all grown to love **Rose Marie,** and we know from her work on *The Dick Van Dyke Show* that she certainly has the recipe to make people laugh. When she visited *Hour's* kitchen, she presented this tasty salad and actually taught me how to "peel" my broccoli. Whether or not you succeed in peeling your broccoli, you'll enjoy this salad.

Cold Broccoli Salad

2–3 bunches broccoli
    Salt
3–4 cloves garlic, chopped
½–¾ cup olive oil
    Lawry's garlic salt
    Juice of 1 lemon
1–2 lemons, for garnish

Peel broccoli stems back to flowerets and cut off bottoms, which are hard and white. Separate broccoli into flowerets. Cook in salted boiling water for 10 minutes—make sure broccoli is crispy, not overcooked. Cool, cover with plastic wrap and refrigerate until cold.

When ready to serve, brown chopped garlic in olive oil and pour over *cold* broccoli. Sprinkle a little Lawry's garlic salt over all, then the lemon juice. Slice lemons and put around platter to decorate.

Serves 6–9.

ROSE MARIE

ONE of the most popular guests on *Hour Magazine* is **Victoria Principal,** Pamela Ewing on *Dallas.* She told us about *The Body Principal* and *The Beauty Principal,* and explained her exercise program for life. Hand in hand with this program go Victoria's "principles," including the 30-day diet for life. Naturally, she encourages us to eat salads—lots of them.

"Eat All You Want" Salad

Onions
Radishes
Turkey
Red cabbage
Cucumbers
Lettuce, several types
Low-calorie salad dressing

Use as much of the vegetable ingredients above as you wish. Top with a low-calorie dressing. Eat until you feel full.

Serves 1.

VICTORIA PRINCIPAL

Quick Molasses Bread

2 cups whole-wheat flour
½ cup soy flour
½ teaspoon cinnamon
¼ teaspoon salt
2 teaspoons baking powder
2 eggs
¼ cup oil
¼ cup molasses
3 tablespoons honey
1 teaspoon grated orange peel
¾ cup milk

Preheat oven to 375°. Stir together whole-wheat and soy flours, cinnamon, salt and baking powder. In another bowl, beat eggs together with oil, molasses, honey, orange peel and milk. Stir liquid mixture into dry ingredients and carefully combine. Batter will be stiff. Turn into a greased 8 x 4 x 2-inch loaf pan. Bake for 30 minutes, or until wood toothpick inserted in center comes out clean.

Makes 1 loaf.

TIM REID

L AST year, First Lady **Nancy Reagan** came to *Hour Magazine* to
present a five-part series with me, on children and drugs. Now, we
all know that she's gracious and cordial, but what impressed us most
was her warmth and genuineness; as soon as she came to the studio,
she pulled out some homemade cookies and handed them out to
the crew and staff. Knowing that cooking is close to her heart, I
asked her to submit a favorite recipe. She chose Monkey Bread.

Monkey Bread

1 ⅗-ounce cake compressed yeast, *or* 1 package dry yeast
1–1¼ cups milk
3 eggs
3 tablespoons granulated sugar
1 teaspoon salt
3½ cups all-purpose flour
1½ sticks (¾ cup) butter, at room temperature
Melted butter

In a bowl, mix the yeast with part of the milk until dissolved. Add 2 eggs
and beat. Then mix in dry ingredients. Add remaining milk a little at a time,
mixing thoroughly, then cut in 1½ sticks butter until thoroughly blended.
Knead the dough, let rise in a warm draft-free place for 1–1½ hours, or until
it doubles in bulk. Knead again, and let rise a second time, 30–40 minutes.

On a floured board, roll dough out into the shape of a log. Cut into 28
equal pieces.

Prepare two 9-inch ring molds by brushing with the melted butter and
dusting with flour. Form each piece of dough into a ball and roll in dish of
melted butter. Place 8–9 balls in the bottom of each ring mold, leaving space
between balls. Then place the remaining balls on top, spacing evenly and di-
viding equally between the two molds.

Let dough rise in a warm, draft-free place. Preheat oven to 375°. Brush
tops of rings with remaining egg (beaten), and bake in preheated oven until
golden, approximately 15 minutes.

Makes 2 9-inch rings.

NANCY REAGAN

Texas Corn Bread

1 cup plain white cornmeal
½ cup self-rising flour
1 teaspoon salt
½ teaspoon baking soda
2 eggs
1 cup buttermilk

Preheat oven to 500°. Mix all ingredients together. Grease a skillet (with ovenproof handle) with some oil, coat lightly with flour. Pour batter into skillet, bake for about 10 minutes, or until golden brown.

Serves 8–10.

MICKEY GILLEY AND MOM, IRENE

Pecan Balls

2 tablespoons granulated sugar
1 stick (½ cup) butter, softened
1 teaspoon vanilla
1 cup pecans, ground
1 cup all-purpose flour
Confectioners' sugar

Preheat oven to 325°. Mix granulated sugar with butter and vanilla. Add nuts and flour. Form into balls. Bake for 15 minutes or so. Roll in confectioners' sugar while still warm. Then roll again in confectioners' sugar.

This recipe is easily doubled or tripled.

Makes about 2½ dozen.

INGA SWENSON

ANYONE who has seen the new, svelte **Lynn Redgrave** would have been as surprised as we were when she visited our show to prepare a banana cream pie. But, guess what? This one's low in calories, because Lynn found it in *Weight Watchers* magazine.

Banana Cream Pie

2 medium bananas
2 tablespoons lemon juice
1 envelope unflavored gelatin
¾ cup warm water
4 slices cinnamon toast, crumbled
½ stick (¼ cup) reduced-calorie margarine, melted
1 tablespoon grated lemon peel
1½ envelopes Equal low-calorie sweetener (equivalent to 3
       teaspoons granulated sugar)
1 cup skim ricotta cheese
1 cup plain low-fat yogurt
2 tablespoons slivered orange peel

Preheat oven to 375°. Slice bananas and mix with lemon juice. Set aside. Sprinkle gelatin over ½ cup warm water in a small bowl. Set aside. In an 8-inch pie plate, combine crumbs with margarine and grated lemon peel. Press into pan to form crust. Bake for 8 minutes. Cool.

Stir remaining ¼ cup warm water into gelatin mixture until gelatin is completely dissolved. Puree three-quarters of the bananas in a food processor or blender. Add Equal, gelatin, ricotta and yogurt. Pour into crust and garnish with remaining bananas. Chill for 4 hours. Top with slivered orange peel.

Serves 6.

PRESENTED BY LYNN REDGRAVE

FOLLOWING in the footsteps of Wally Amos, **Dale Robinette** was inspired to create People-Bones Chocolate Chip Cookies—delicious chocolate chip cookies in the shape of dog biscuits. Once we got over our initial reaction to their shape, the staff and I loved them. In fact, they were almost as big a hit as Bert Greene's Chicken Dog. (See page 142.)

People-Bones Chocolate Chip Cookies

2 sticks (1 cup) margarine
1 cup granulated sugar
3 eggs
3 cups all-purpose flour
2 teaspoons baking powder
1 teaspoon nutmeg, or your own favorite spice
Pinch salt
1 cup mini chocolate chips

Glaze

4 tablespoons confectioners' sugar
1 teaspoon vanilla
¼ cup milk
¼ teaspoon salt
⅔ stick butter or margarine, melted

Preheat oven to 350°. Mix 2 sticks margarine, granulated sugar and eggs until smooth. Gradually add dry ingredients, then chips. Lightly flour rolling pin and flat surface or pastry board. Roll out dough ¼ inch thick and cut out bone shapes. (If the kids have been cuttin' up and are in the doghouse, let them cut some fun shapes—they'll be quiet as mice.) Arrange cookies on a lightly greased baking sheet. Bake for 10–12 minutes, or until lightly golden.

Mix together all glaze ingredients and spread glaze on warm cookies—*bone appétit!*

Makes about 24 medium cookies.

DALE ROBINETTE

Printed by permission of People-Bones. Copyright © 1982 by People-Bones, P.O. Box 605, Topanga, CA 90290.

Rudy Stanish Chocolate Roll

6 ounces chocolate bits, melted
2 tablespoons strong brewed coffee
5 eggs, separated
1 cup granulated sugar
2–3 tablespoons oil
   Cocoa powder

Filling

1 pint heavy cream
3 tablespoons granulated sugar
6 grains salt

Preheat oven to 350°. Mix chocolate and coffee together. Beat egg whites and ¼ cup sugar until stiff. In a separate bowl, beat egg yolks and ¾ cup sugar together. Fold chocolate into egg yolk mixture, then fold in beaten egg whites. Fold as much air into mixture as possible.

Oil sides and bottom of a jelly-roll pan. Line bottom of pan with waxed paper. Coat waxed paper with oil. Place batter in pan and bake for 17 minutes. Remove from oven and sprinkle with cocoa powder. Put two overlapping pieces of wax paper on top of cake, turn over and remove pan.

Whip cream; beat in the 3 tablespoons sugar and the salt. Put whipped cream in center of cooled cake and spread evenly. Slowly roll cake toward you, using waxed paper. As one piece of waxed paper ends, the other should be there to continue the rolling process. Place roll on serving dish, seam side down.

Serves 6–8.

NANETTE FABRAY

WHAT can I say about the next recipe, presented by the woman with whom I share my life? Aside from being a mother, an actress, a spokesperson for many charities and a former Miss America, **Mary Ann Mobley** is my wife. She's made me happier than I could ever imagine and is more than just my bread and butter—she's my cup of tea! This recipe was given to her by two dear friends of ours, Leon and Charles, who live in Cleveland, Mississippi.

Mary Ann says: "If guests suddenly appear, I run to the kitchen and prepare this, and people think I've been slaving. It's so simple, my teenaged daughter can prepare it. My schedule is such that I don't have time to prepare long, involved dishes, but I love to entertain and have friends over. This is a wonderful dessert I can cook in 10 minutes if someone drops by. I always have everything on hand—butter, milk, sugar, self-rising flour and if I don't have fresh peaches, I use canned, and it tastes exactly the same. You serve it hot. I just dish it out and put ice cream on top, or serve it as is. It's not bad cold either!"

Peach Cobbler

6–8 large, very ripe fresh peaches, peeled, *or* 1 large can sliced
     cling peaches
1–2 cups granulated sugar
 1 stick (½ cup) butter
 1 cup self-rising flour
 1 cup milk
    Vanilla ice cream (optional)

Preheat oven to 400°. If you are using fresh peaches, peel, pit and slice thin. Put in plastic bowl and pour 1 cup sugar over them. Stir well. Cover tightly and place in refrigerator for 2 hours. Canned peaches are used as is.

Place butter in bottom of rectangular Pyrex baking dish about 11¾ x 7½ x 1¾-inches deep. Put in oven until butter melts. In a bowl, mix the flour, 1 cup sugar and the milk. Beat well with a whisk. Pour mixture over melted butter (don't mix), and spoon peaches over batter mixture. If you are using canned peaches, add only a small amount of juice from the can. If using fresh peaches, use natural juice. VERY IMPORTANT: *Do not stir peaches into batter.* Bake until top becomes golden brown (the cake mixture comes up around the peaches). Serve hot. Top with vanilla ice cream, if desired.

Serves 9–12.

MARY ANN MOBLEY

ACADEMY Award-winning actress, activist, producer, fitness guru—there are so many ways to describe **Jane Fonda.** But for me, there is one description that fits best—energetic! So on her last visit she made—what else?—a healthful energy drink. Obviously it works. Jane Fonda *is* energy!

Energy Drink

6 ice cubes
½ cup nonfat milk
½ cup unsweetened apple juice
½ papaya
½ cup strawberries (peaches or any fruit)
¼ cup wheat germ or bran
½ banana
¼ cup protein powder

Put everything in blender and mix well. Amounts of all ingredients can be altered to suit your own taste.

Serves 1.

JANE FONDA

Reprinted by permission of Simon & Schuster, Inc., from *Women Coming of Age* by Jane Fonda with Mignon McCarthy, copyright © 1984 by Jane Fonda.

3

HOUR REGULAR COOKS IN THE KITCHEN

Over the years, we have had a tendency to rely on certain dependables. On the following pages, you'll get just a sampling of some of the special dishes offered by the guests we call our "regular" *Hour Magazine* cooks. I can tell you from experience, you can't miss with these recipes!

WHEN **Myra Chanin** first released her recipe for cheesecake, she became the talk of Philadelphia, and now she's called Mother Wonderful by practically everyone. Over the years, Myra's presented her recipe for gefilte fish and other traditional Jewish dishes, but everyone's favorite here at the studio is definitely her cheesecake. When I think about it, besides learning some trade secrets about cooking from Myra, I've learned more Yiddish words from her than from any other guest in the history of *Hour Magazine*. But you don't have to be Jewish to love her cooking! Here are two of my favorites, which Myra's made on the show.

Triple Chocolate Cheesecake

Crust

- ¼ pound lightly salted butter
- 2 cups very finely ground crumbs from Nabisco Famous Chocolate Wafers*
- ¼ cup granulated sugar

Filling

- 3½ ounces Maillard's Eagle sweet chocolate or Baker's German's sweet chocolate
- 4 8-ounce packages cream cheese
- 1¼ cups granulated sugar
- 1 tablespoon Myers's rum
- 1½ teaspoons Wagner's vanilla extract
  Pinch of salt
- 4 large eggs
- ¼ cup Guittard's chocolate chips, *or* 2 ounces of Maillard's Eagle sweet chocolate or Baker's German's sweet chocolate, chopped in a food processor into chip-size bits

Topping

- 2 cups sour cream
- ¼ cup granulated sugar
- 1 teaspoon Wagner's almond extract

* No other chocolate cookie crumbles with quite the same consistency.

Preheat oven to 350°. Melt butter over very low heat. Combine butter with crumbs and ¼ cup sugar in food processor until well blended (or combine in a plastic container, using a fork). Press mixture over bottom and up sides of an ungreased 10-inch springform pan. There should be enough to coat the entire pan.

To prepare filling, melt 3½ ounces chocolate over simmering water in top of double boiler, in a pan over a Flame Tamer or in a microwave oven. Set aside. In a mixer bowl, combine cream cheese and 1¼ cups sugar, and beat for 2 minutes, or until soft—the cream cheese need not be at room temperature. Add rum, vanilla, melted chocolate, salt, and blend thoroughly. The eggs need not be at room temperature either. Add the eggs, one at a time, keeping the mixer on the *lowest* speed in order to prevent too much air from destroying the proper consistency of the batter; mix just until each egg has been incorporated into the batter. Stir in chocolate bits. Pour filling into the crust and bake in preheated oven for 40 minutes. If ingredients were not at room temperature, add 5 minutes to the baking time. Remove from oven and let stand on counter top for 10 minutes while you prepare topping. *This is a very essential step.*

Topping: Combine sour cream, ¼ cup sugar and almond extract in a plastic bowl, using a rubber spatula. Spread evenly over top of baked filling and return cheesecake to 350° oven for 10 minutes. Remove from oven and place in refrigerator to cool *immediately.* This prevents cracks from forming in the cheesecake.

Note

This cheesecake does not freeze well.

Serves 8

MYRA CHANIN

Reprinted by permission of Bantam Books Inc., from *Mother Wonderful's Book of Cheesecakes and Other Goodies,* copyright © 1981 by Myra Chanin.

Sylvia Daskell's Golden Chicken Soup

My own wonderful mother, Sylvia Daskell, gave me this recipe for her chicken soup.

   1 3-pound chicken
6–8 extra chicken feet
   5 cups boiling water
   1 medium onion, peeled
   2 stalks celery, cut into 3-inch pieces

1 carrot, peeled
1 parsley root with greens attached, peeled and cut in half
    lengthwise
Salt and white pepper to taste
Fresh dill (optional)

Clean chicken and feet. Place in bottom of a soup kettle. Cover with boiling water. You do not want to add too much water or the soup will not have enough flavor. Add onion, celery and carrot. Bring liquid in pot to a boil and then lower heat to simmer. A half hour later, add parsley root and continue to cook. Chicken should be soft in about 1 hour.

Remove chicken and feet and vegetables from pot. Strain broth, cool and skim off fat. Remove chicken meat from bones and return some meat to the broth, if desired. Reheat soup and add salt and white pepper to taste. Sprinkle with fresh dill.

Serves 3–4.

MYRA CHANIN

THERE'S an old adage that "too many cooks mess up the minestrone," and so, from the inception of *Hour Magazine*, we chose just one cook who would appear weekly, every Monday. Of course you all know **Laurie Burrows Grad,** whose contributions to the show and "Make It Easy" segments have certainly been among the most valuable additions to *Hour*. Laurie has an uncanny ability to make even a simple meal look elegant! Her weekly suggestions are practical, achievable and clear, and when she says she makes it easy, you know she does. For me, she makes the taping for the Monday show easy, but more important, enjoyable!

Zucchini Pancakes

These small round variations on the potato pancake make a wonderful brunch dish topped with sour cream and chives, or they can be served as a side dish with roast meats or poultry.

3 cups (1½ pounds) grated zucchini
4 eggs
½ cup all-purpose flour
½ cup freshly grated Parmesan cheese
½ cup mayonnaise
¼ cup finely chopped scallions, both green and white parts

1   teaspoon lemon juice
    Salt and freshly ground black pepper to taste
2   tablespoons vegetable oil (or more)
1   tablespoon butter
    Sour cream
    Chopped chives or scallion greens

Place grated zucchini between layers of paper towels and blot dry. In a large bowl, combine zucchini with eggs, flour, Parmesan, mayonnaise, scallions, lemon juice, salt and pepper to taste; mix until a smooth batter is formed. On a griddle, or in a large skillet, heat oil and butter, and spoon out 2 tablespoons of the batter for each pancake. Brown well on each side for 2 minutes, flattening out second side with spatula. Drain for a minute on paper towels to remove excess grease. Repeat with remaining batter, adding more oil and butter as necessary.

Serve hot with sour cream and chives.

Variations

Pancakes can be topped with Italian tomato sauce and grated Parmesan cheese, or served Mexican style with guacamole, sour cream and salsa.

Makes about 24 pancakes.

LAURIE BURROWS GRAD

Reprinted by permission of Laurie Burrows Grad from *Make It Easy Entertaining*. Los Angeles: Jeremy P. Tarcher, Inc., 1984.

Marinated Oriental Beef and Pepper Salad

This salad is a great way to use up leftover meat—roast beef, steak or even pot roast. It's great as a main-course salad on a hot summer night, or a winner for your next luncheon!

3   cups rare roast beef, steak or other cooked beef, cut into
        2 x 1-inch strips
1   green pepper, cut into thin julienne strips
2   tomatoes, cut into small wedges
3   scallions, minced, both green and white parts
½   cup mushrooms, sliced (optional)
½   cup jicama (a Mexican vegetable) cut in julienne strips, *or*
        ½ cup sliced water chestnuts (optional)

Marinade

½ cup teriyaki sauce
3 tablespoons peanut oil
3 tablespoons Japanese rice wine vinegar or white wine vinegar
1½ teaspoons freshly grated ginger, *or* 1 teaspoon ground ginger
⅓ cup dry sherry
2 tablespoons oriental sesame oil

4 cups mixed greens: leaf lettuce, red lettuce, romaine

In a large bowl, place beef, green pepper, tomatoes, scallions, mushrooms and jicama or water chestnuts. Combine marinade ingredients in screw-top jar and shake until smooth. Pour marinade over meat and vegetables and toss well. Cover and refrigerate for 3 hours.

At serving time, drain off excess marinade, line a large salad bowl with the mixed greens, place marinated meat and vegetables on top. Serve immediately, accompanied by toasted pita bread.

Make It Easy Tips

Rare roast beef is generally available at delicatessens. Ask for about a pound of the rarest meat and slice it into strips at home.

A serrated tomato or bread knife is an invaluable tool for cutting tomatoes.

Serves 4–6.

LAURIE BURROWS GRAD

Reprinted by permission of Laurie Burrows Grad from *Make It Easy in Your Kitchen*. Los Angeles: Jeremy P. Tarcher, Inc., 1982.

B ERT Greene and all-American cooking go hand in hand. I love his visits to *Hour's* kitchen. He's funny and gracious, and loves his food. Bert's responsible for the recipe that more people in more cities have asked me about. It's Chicken Dog, and I have to admit in fairness to Bert that it wasn't the taste that offended me, I had an "image" problem with the name. It really wasn't that bad! Anyhow, Bert swears by it, and suggests that pronouncing the name with a drawl—Chicken D . . . a . . . w . . . g—may help a bit.

Chicken Dog

1⅓ cups milk, scalded
7 tablespoons butter
2 cups soft bread crumbs
2 cups chopped cooked chicken
2 eggs, lightly beaten
1 tablespoon chopped fresh parsley
2 teaspoons chopped fresh tarragon
1 tablespoon grated onion
½ teaspoon salt
¼ teaspoon freshly ground pepper
2 tablespoons all-purpose flour
½ cup milk
½ cup chicken stock
½ cup sour cream
Salt and pepper to taste

Preheat oven to 375°. Pour scalded milk into large bowl. Add 5 tablespoons butter; let melt. Add bread crumbs, chicken, eggs, parsley, tarragon, onion, ½ teaspoon salt and ¼ teaspoon pepper. Mix thoroughly. Pat mixture into a well-buttered loaf pan. Place loaf pan in roasting pan; pour enough boiling water around the loaf pan to come halfway up the sides. Bake 1 hour.

Remove loaf pan from oven. Carefully pour off any juices; reserve. Unmold loaf onto a platter. Keep warm. Remove excess fat from juices. Melt remaining 2 tablespoons butter in a medium saucepan over medium-low heat. Stir in flour; cook 2 minutes. Add meat juices, ½ cup milk and the stock. Simmer until slightly thickened. Remove from heat. Stir in sour cream. Add salt and pepper to taste. Serve gravy with loaf.

Serves 6–8.

BERT GREENE

Reprinted by permission of Contemporary Books, Inc., from *Honest American Fare* by Bert Greene. Copyright © 1981 by Bert Greene.

Red Pepper Cheese Bread

    1 large red bell pepper
    1 package Fleischmann's dry yeast
    3 cups all-purpose flour (approximately)
 1½ cups stone-ground whole-wheat flour
    1 teaspoon light brown sugar
    2 teaspoons salt
  ⅛ teaspoon cayenne pepper
    1 teaspoon crushed dried hot red pepper
    1 teaspoon sesame seeds
    1 teaspoon fennel seeds
    1 teaspoon anise seeds
  ¼ cup lukewarm milk
 1¼ cups lukewarm water
    1 cup grated Monterey Jack cheese
    1 tablespoon unsalted butter, melted

Roast the bell pepper over a gas flame until charred all over (or place under broiler until charred). Carefully wrap pepper in paper towels and place in a plastic bag. Let stand until cool. Rub the charred skin from the pepper with paper towels. Core the pepper; chop fine.

Place the yeast in the bowl of an electric mixer with a dough hook attachment. Add 2 cups all-purpose flour, the whole-wheat flour, brown sugar, salt, cayenne pepper, hot red pepper, sesame, fennel and anise seeds. Turn mixer on low and add milk and water. When batter is mixed, add the chopped red bell pepper and cheese. Put mixture on high for 5 minutes. Transfer dough to a floured board. Knead dough, adding the remaining 1 cup all-purpose flour, until elastic, about 5 minutes. Divide dough in half; roll each half into long French- or Italian-style loaves. Place in French-bread pans. Cover with a flour-rubbed tea towel. Let stand until dough doubles in bulk, 1–1½ hours.

Preheat oven to 400°. Gently slash the top of each loaf lengthwise with a razor blade. Brush with melted butter. Place a roasting pan half-filled with water in the bottom of the oven. Place bread on shelf in top third of oven; bake 12 minutes. Reduce oven heat to 325° and continue to bake 35 minutes longer. Cool on a rack.

Makes 2 loaves.

BERT GREENE

Reprinted by permission of Workman Publishing Co., Inc., from *Greene on Greens* by Bert Greene. Copyright © 1984 by Bert Greene.

MARGO Kidushim owns her own produce market, so she specializes in fruits and vegetables. She has the ability to take simple fruits and vegetables and incorporate them in unique dishes, such as her Apple-filled Squash, that no other cook could provide for us. But whatever she presents has been a success on our show. We've included her recipe for Moussaka, too. It's a good one—trust me!

Moussaka

Serve with a salad and crunchy French bread for a perfect meal!

    1 large eggplant
    1 teaspoon salt
    2 cups cooking oil
    2 medium-size onions, chopped
    2 pounds ground beef, *or* 1 pound ground beef and 1 pound
         ground lamb
    4 fresh medium-size tomatoes, chopped
    1 small can tomato paste
  ½ cup chopped fresh parsley
    1 teaspoon marjoram
    2 teaspoons oregano
    3 cloves fresh garlic, minced fine
    1 teaspoon salt
    1 teaspoon pepper
    4 tablespoons butter
    4 tablespoons all-purpose flour
  ½ teaspoon salt
1½ cups milk
    2 eggs, beaten
  ½ cup grated Parmesan cheese
    1 cup dry seasoned bread crumbs

Peel eggplant and slice in ½-inch-thick slices. Place in bowl and cover with water to which 1 teaspoon salt has been added. Place plate on top of eggplant to force it under water and let soak 20–30 minutes. Drain eggplant and pat dry. Fry in oil until transparent. You may also broil it, but watch closely so it does not burn. Either way, be sure to pierce eggplant all over with a fork. This permits it to cook faster. If frying, drain on paper towels. Pour fat out of frying pan. Add onion and meat to pan, and fry until lightly browned. Add fresh tomatoes, tomato paste, parsley, marjoram, oregano, garlic, 1 teaspoon salt and the pepper. Stir and simmer 20–30 minutes.

Meanwhile, preheat oven to 325°. Melt butter in saucepan. Blend in flour to form a paste, then add ½ teaspoon salt. Add milk slowly. Cook, stirring constantly until mixture thickens, approximately 3 minutes. Add a little sauce to beaten eggs to warm them, then pour all the eggs into white sauce and mix to blend. Add cheese.

Sprinkle seasoned bread crumbs across bottom of 11 x 13-inch baking dish. Now layer as follows: eggplant, meat sauce, eggplant, cheese sauce. Bake 1 hour, or until lightly browned. Let rest 10 minutes before cutting.

Serves 6–8.

MARGO KIDUSHIM

Apple-filled Squash

1 stick (½ cup) butter
3 apples (Granny Smith preferred), peeled, cored and diced
1 teaspoon ground cinnamon
½ teaspoon ground nutmeg
¼ cup brown sugar, firmly packed
¼ cup pineapple juice
3 small Gold Nugget squash, cut in half and seeds removed
⅓ cup chopped pecans

Preheat oven to 375°. Melt butter in medium-size frying pan over low heat. Add apples, spices and brown sugar. Stir in the pineapple juice, then sauté, watching carefully, until the apples are fork tender—but *not* mushy. Remove from heat and cool.

Meanwhile place squash, cut side down, in a shallow baking dish. Into dish, pour hot water ½-inch deep. Cover well with foil and bake squash for 30 minutes, or until fork tender.

Remove cooked squash from dish. Turn right side up and fill cavities with apples. Sprinkle with pecans. Broil until lightly browned. Serve immediately. A great accompaniment to ham or lamb.

Serves 6.

MARGO KIDUSHIM

Easy Beef Béarnaise

    1 teaspoon dry tarragon
    1 tablespoon white wine vinegar
    ½ teaspoon ground pepper
       Pinch of cayenne pepper
    2 tablespoons lemon juice
       Salt to taste
    2 tablespoons butter
    ⅓ medium onion, chopped
    1 filet mignon (2–3 pounds), sliced into ¾-inch-thick slices
    ¼ cup white wine
    ¼ cup low-fat milk
    1 can golden mushroom soup

Before guests arrive, measure and combine in cup tarragon, vinegar, pepper, cayenne, lemon juice and salt. Refrigerate.

Melt butter in an electric fry pan or skillet over medium-high heat. Add onion and cook until golden. Add beef slices and brown on both sides. Reduce heat to medium, remove beef to a warmed plate. Swirl wine in pan. Add low-fat milk and the golden mushroom soup, stirring constantly. When sauce is simmering and smooth, add the vinegar-lemon juice seasoning mixture. Stir sauce and bring to simmer. Return beef to skillet, cook 3 minutes. Turn over slices, reduce heat to very low, cover and leave until ready to serve.

Serves 4–6.

JACKIE OLDEN

Avocado and Orange Salad

1 avocado, sliced
1 cucumber, peeled and sliced
1 head butter lettuce, torn into pieces
2 tablespoons chopped green onion
1 11-ounce can mandarin oranges, drained

Dressing

½ cup oil
¼ cup orange juice
2 tablespoons granulated sugar
2 tablespoons red wine vinegar
1 tablespoon lemon juice
½ teaspoon grated orange peel
¼ teaspoon salt

In a salad bowl, combine avocado, cucumber, lettuce, onion and mandarin oranges. Mix all the dressing ingredients together and pour over salad just before serving.

Serves 4.

JACKIE OLDEN

HE'S a master chef, born in Stuttgart, Germany, who spent over twenty years mastering cuisines from around the world. **Chef Tell** has been awarded the Cordon Bleu award four times, owns his own gourmet restaurant in Philadelphia and is familiar to us because of his 90-second spots on *PM Magazine,* where he managed to present the most intricate meals in less time than it takes me to introduce him. While I was in Philadelphia doing a show for Group W some years ago, I had the pleasure of dining at his restaurant one night. I went with my executive producer, Marty Berman, and my producer, Steve Clements, and we had the dinner we all refer to as the best meal of our lives! We ate and laughed in style! How do you make cooking funny? Chef Tell knows. When he visits *Hour's* kitchen, he never fails to win me over with his offbeat and wacky sense of humor, which surfaces unexpectedly and causes explosive laughter in the audience.

Chicken Pompadour and Sauce Hollandaise

6 pieces boneless chicken breast, skinned
Salt and freshly ground pepper to taste
2 eggs
Flour for dredging
2 cups blanched, chopped almonds
6 tablespoons butter or margarine

Lightly pound the chicken breasts to even thickness. Season with salt and pepper. Beat the eggs in a flat soup plate. Put a good amount of flour on a piece of waxed paper. Put the almonds on another piece of waxed paper. Dredge each chicken breast in the flour, dip it into the egg and then coat it with the almonds. Press with the palm of your hand so that the almonds stick to the chicken. Melt the butter in a large frying pan and sauté the chicken breasts for 4–5 minutes on each side, or until cooked through and golden brown. Serve immediately with Sauce Hollandaise (see below).

Sauce Hollandaise

8 ounces clarified butter (see below)
6 egg yolks
½ cup dry white wine
Salt and freshly ground black pepper to taste

Clarified Butter: Put 1 pound of unsalted butter in a small saucepan and melt it over high heat. As it bubbles, a foam will come to the surface. When this foam subsides and sinks to the bottom of the pan, pour off the clear butter on the top—this is your clarified butter.

Put the egg yolks and wine into a heavy saucepan. Beat together over medium heat until the mixture is thickened. Remove from heat and continue to beat until the mixture cools a little. Using a wire whisk, beat in the clarified butter, until the ingredients are well combined. Season with salt and pepper. Do not reheat the sauce; if you have to keep it warm, place it over a pot of hot water.

Note

If you are hesitant about putting the saucepan directly over the heat, you can combine the egg yolks and wine in the top of a double boiler over gently boiling water. Remember, too, that the egg yolk mixture and the clarified butter should be at about the same temperature (140°) to combine properly.

Serves 6, about 2 cups sauce.

CHEF TELL

Printed by permission of Chef Tell Quick Cuisine. Copyright © 1982 by Chef Tell.

Black Forest Apples

8 apples
8 tablespoons raisins
8 tablespoons sliced almonds
8 tablespoons honey
8 tablespoons kirsch (optional)

Preheat the oven to 350°. Cut a lid off each of the apples and reserve. Peel each apple one-third of the way down. Core with a melon-ball cutter, being careful not to cut through the bottom of the apple. Fill each apple with 1 tablespoon each of raisins and almonds. Pour 1 tablespoon honey into each apple and sprinkle 1 tablespoon kirsch over each. Put the tops back on the apples. Put the apples into a baking pan and pour in about ¼ inch of water. Bake for 25 minutes, or until the apples are tender.

Serves 8.

CHEF TELL

Printed by permission of Chef Tell Quick Cuisine. Copyright © 1982 by Chef Tell.

4

RECIPE CONTEST WINNERS

In response to the continued requests for recipes and the interest generated by our cooking segments, we started something new in 1984; we decided to conduct our own recipe contest. I asked viewers to send in their families' favorite recipes for a chance to become a winner in the *Hour* recipe contest. Thousands of postcards flooded the studio within weeks. Over a five-day period on the show, I selected twenty-five recipes at random and turned them over to a panel of cooking experts who regularly appear on the program. Each recipe was tested by members of the panel, and five winners were selected for an all-expense-paid trip to Hollywood and an opportunity to prepare their winning dishes for me on the show.

Naturally our winners were all enthusiastic, but I was amazed that they were so poised facing the television cameras and studio audience. They may have been amateurs on television, but that certainly didn't affect their skills as cooks! In fact, one winner, Peggy Huffman, was so excited and animated that we sent a crew out to her home in Pineville, West Virginia, the day the show aired. Pineville named the day of our visit Peggy Huffman Day in her honor.

When we offered the winning recipes to our viewers, we received over 125,000 requests for them! And when we announced the 1985 recipe contest, we received well over 50,000 entries. Hundreds of people sent their recipes in by Federal Express so as not to miss our deadline. And some enterprising cooks even made their recipes for me—and sent the food. It's obvious that America loves to cook. On the next few pages, you'll find the winning recipes from the past two years.

Barbecue Spareribs

4 pounds country-style pork ribs
  Water
1 small onion, chopped
2–3 apples, sliced

Barbecue Sauce

½ small onion, chopped
2 tablespoons butter
1 pinch celery seed
1 small clove garlic, minced
1 small pinch cayenne pepper
1 cup Heinz catsup
1 cup water
4 tablespoons brown sugar
1–2 tablespoons apple cider vinegar

Place spareribs in Dutch oven or wok. Add enough water to cover spareribs. Heat to boiling; reduce heat, cover and simmer 40 minutes; drain. Preheat oven to 375°. Line bottom of clay pot with half the chopped onion and half the apples. Place spareribs in pot and add rest of onion and apples. Roast in preheated oven for 40 minutes.

To make barbecue sauce, sauté chopped onion in butter in saucepan. Add celery seed, garlic and cayenne; then add catsup and 1 cup water. Add brown sugar and vinegar; simmer sauce over low heat for about ½ hour. (I use this sauce for chicken or pork or over meatloaf, too.)

Remove spareribs and place on side in broiler pan. Brush with barbecue sauce and put under broiler for the last 5 minutes.

Serves 6.

LINDA LACKAS
FROM RUBICON, WISCONSIN

Sweet-and-Sour Chicken

Garlic salt to taste
2 pounds chicken, cut into bite-size pieces
¼ cup vinegar
2 tablespoons brown sugar
¼ teaspoon salt
¼ teaspoon ginger
¼ cup catsup
1 tablespoon soy sauce
2 teaspoons cornstarch
1 large can pineapple chunks, drained (save juice)
1 medium whole tomato
1 medium green pepper, diced
Hot cooked rice

Sprinkle garlic salt over chicken and pan fry until brown. Set aside. In a saucepan, combine vinegar, brown sugar, salt, ginger, catsup, soy sauce, cornstarch and pineapple juice. Simmer sauce until thick. Return chicken to heat and add sauce, tomato, pepper and pineapple. Simmer over low heat until heated through, about 25–30 minutes. Serve over rice.

Serves 4.

KATHY SPIESS
FROM PEORIA, ARIZONA

Dijon Shrimp à la Santa Cruz

4 tablespoons butter
4 tablespoons peanut oil
4–6 cloves garlic, minced
Juice of 1 lemon
½ teaspoon Worcestershire sauce
½ teaspoon Dijon mustard, or ¼ teaspoon dry mustard
1 pound shrimp, peeled and deveined

Melt butter. Blend in all other ingredients, except shrimp, to make sauce. Marinate shrimp in sauce for 2–3 hours.
Preheat broiler to 450°. Broil shrimp for 5 minutes. Turn, broil 2–3

minutes, or until done. Remove shrimp to serving dish; pour warmed sauce over top.

Serves 4.

NANCY LEE GILLESPIE
FROM SANTA CRUZ, CALIFORNIA

Corn Pone Bitties or Cornmeal Puffs

1½ cups yellow cornmeal (stone-ground is better)
1 cup all-purpose flour
1 tablespoon granulated sugar
2 teaspoons double-acting baking powder
1½ teaspoons salt
¼ teaspoon cayenne pepper
1 cup milk
2 large eggs, separated, at room temperature
¾ stick (6 tablespoons) unsalted butter, melted and cooled
Vegetable shortening
Pinch of cream of tartar
Pinch of salt

Preheat oven to 450°. Sift together cornmeal, flour, sugar, baking powder, 1½ teaspoons salt and the cayenne. Set aside. In another bowl, combine milk, egg yolks and the cooled butter. Add sifted dry ingredients and stir batter until it is just combined. Grease 3 muffin tins (36 ⅛-cup-capacity muffin cups, in all) with shortening, and heat them in preheated oven for 3 minutes.
In a bowl, beat egg whites until they are foamy, add cream of tartar and pinch of salt, beat until whites hold stiff peaks. Fold the whites into batter, spoon heaping tablespoons into each hot muffin tin and bake puffs in hot oven for 12–15 minutes, or until they are golden. Invert onto racks and transfer to serving dish while still warm.

Makes 36 delicious puffs.

MAGGI J. MONTGOMERY
FROM SUN CITY, CALIFORNIA

Russian Corn Bread

3 cups self-rising cornmeal
2 tablespoons granulated sugar
½ cup oil
1 cup chopped onion
½ cup shredded cheese
3 average-size hot peppers, chopped
1 8-ounce can cream-style corn
2 eggs, beaten
2 cups buttermilk

Preheat oven to 425°. Combine all ingredients except eggs and buttermilk. Add eggs and buttermilk. Stir. Pour batter into skillet with ovenproof handle. Bake 45–50 minutes.

Note

For best results use a cast-iron skillet that is 4 inches deep.

Serves 10–12.

PEGGY HUFFMAN
FROM PINEVILLE, WEST VIRGINIA

Mexican Fruitcake

Fruitcake

1 20-ounce can crushed pineapple, undrained
2 cups all-purpose flour
2 teaspoons baking soda
2 cups granulated sugar
2 eggs
1 cup chopped walnuts or pecans

Cream Cheese Frosting

2 cups confectioners' sugar
1 8-ounce package cream cheese
1 stick (½ cup) margarine, melted
1 teaspoon vanilla

Preheat oven to 350°. Mix fruitcake ingredients together. Pour into a 13 x 9-inch pan greased with margarine and bake 45 minutes (35 minutes if using glass baking dish).

Blend frosting ingredients until smooth and frost cake while still warm. This is delicious, and so easy and fast.

Serves 12.

PEGGY HUFFMAN
FROM PINEVILLE, WEST VIRGINIA

Coastal Crustacean Rounds

    3 ounces cream cheese, softened
    4 tablespoons margarine, softened
    5 dashes Tabasco sauce
    1 cup grated Cheddar cheese
    1 4-ounce can green chilies, drained and chopped
    1 4¼-ounce can small shrimp, drained
    6 ounces white crab meat, drained and flaked
    ⅔ cup sour cream
    ⅓ cup grated Cheddar cheese
    ¼ teaspoon salt
    1 package party rye bread, or 1 box melba toast rounds
       Paprika

Preheat oven to 350°. Place softened cream cheese, margarine, Tabasco and 1 cup grated cheese into mixing bowl. Blend well and add the chilies, shrimp and crab. Stir and set aside.

In small bowl, combine sour cream, ⅓ cup grated Cheddar and the salt. Spread a spoonful of the seafood mixture on each bread or toast round. Top each by spreading an equal amount of the sour cream mixture over the seafood mixture. Sprinkle with paprika. Bake on a baking sheet about 15 minutes. Serve hot.

Makes about 3 dozen hors d'oeuvres.

SUSAN W. PAJCIC
FROM JACKSONVILLE, FLORIDA

Carrot Chowder

   1 pound hamburger
 ½ teaspoon salt
 ⅓ cup chopped celery
 ⅓ cup chopped onion
 ½ cup diced green pepper
   4 cups tomato juice
1½ cups water
   2 cans cream of celery soup
2½ cups grated carrots
   1 teaspoon granulated sugar
 ½ teaspoon garlic salt
 ½ teaspoon pepper
 ⅛ teaspoon ground marjoram
   Swiss cheese slices

Brown hamburger and drain off fat. Add salt, celery, onion and green pepper. Cover and simmer on low heat until vegetables are tender, about 10 minutes.

In large saucepan, combine remaining ingredients. Bring mixture to boil. Turn down heat, add hamburger mixture and simmer 30 minutes. Serve over slices of Swiss cheese.

Serves 8.

MELANIE ZIMMERMAN
FROM ALPINE, UTAH

Carrot and Pineapple King Cole Slaw

 ⅔ cup mayonnaise
 ⅔ cup sour cream
   1 teaspoon grated onion
   1 tablespoon lemon juice
   1 teaspoon granulated sugar
   Pinch of salt
   1 can pineapple chunks, well drained
   1 cup shredded carrots

2 cups shredded cabbage
⅓ cup toasted almonds, slivered

Blend together mayonnaise, sour cream, onion, lemon juice and sugar. Add pinch of salt. Combine pineapple, carrots, cabbage and almonds in a large bowl. Add mayonnaise mixture and toss well. Chill.

Serves 6.

MARIANNE PEARCE
FROM NEW HAVEN, ILLINOIS

Quick 'n' Easy Chicken Delight

2 whole chicken breasts, boned
Pinch tarragon
Salt and pepper to taste
2 tablespoons butter
8 ounces fresh mushrooms or seedless grapes
1 packet McCormick chicken gravy mix
1 cup half-and-half
1 tablespoon dried or fresh parsley
1 tablespoon sherry

Cut boneless breasts into 1-inch strips, sprinkle with tarragon and salt and pepper. Heat butter in heavy skillet. Sauté meat until it turns white, remove to a warmed serving dish and keep warm. Add mushrooms or grapes to the pan, and sauté for a few minutes. Blend gravy mix with half-and-half and stir into pan; stir constantly until sauce is thickened. Add parsley and sherry, stir well. Pour over chicken strips.

Serves 4.

JANET SLEVIN
FROM GREAT FALLS, VIRGINIA

Tropical Loaf

    2 cups all-purpose flour
    ¾ cup granulated sugar
    1 teaspoon baking powder
    1 teaspoon baking soda
    ½ teaspoon salt
    1 egg
    ¼ cup vegetable oil
    1 teaspoon vanilla
    1 cup mashed banana
    1 cup crushed pineapple, *not* drained
    1 cup chopped dates (optional)
    ½ cup chopped nuts

Preheat oven to 350°. In a large bowl, thoroughly stir together the flour, sugar, baking powder, baking soda and salt. In a separate bowl, beat egg. Add oil, vanilla, banana and pineapple; mix well. Add to dry ingredients, stirring until well moistened. Fold in dates and nuts. Pour batter into greased pan. Bake in preheated oven for 1 hour (in 5 x 9 x 5¾-inch loaf pan) or 35–45 minutes (in 9 x 9-inch baking pan), or until toothpick inserted in middle comes out clean. Cool 10 minutes in pan, remove from pan and cool completely on wire racks.

Makes 1 loaf.

DEBORAH K. DE WITT
FROM SCRANTON, KANSAS

5

<u>HOUR</u> EXPERTS IN THE KITCHEN

I thought that the *Hour Magazine Cookbook* would not be complete if we didn't ask our experts to participate. So we asked them for their favorite recipes. It certainly allows us to see another side of their personalities. Read on.

No one on *Hour Magazine* has a more devoted following than **Dr. Isadore Rosenfeld**. He's an eminent professor of medicine in the Cardiology Division of New York Hospital–Cornell Medical Center and a world-renowned cardiologist. But I think his real drawing card is his sense of humor and his gracious "bedside" manner. Dr. Rosenfeld, with his insatiable curiosity, never stops learning, and somehow he can take the most complicated medical procedure and explain it to our audience in simple, understandable terms.

In fact he's so popular across the country that there are groups that get together every Wednesday just to watch his medical segments. Where else could you get free medical advice every week?

When I asked him to submit a recipe I was surprised at his choice. However, it arrived with the following disclaimer, "Raisin Loaves is one of my wife's specialties. It's a true breakfast treat for me, but I don't eat it often because, as you can see, the ingredients are *not* recommended by *my* cardiologist."

Raisin Loaves

       1 cup warm milk
       4 tablespoons butter
     1–2 teaspoons salt
     ½ cup granulated sugar
       4 egg yolks, *or* 2 whole eggs (richer with egg yolks)
     ½ cup mashed potatoes
       2 packages dry yeast
     ¼ cup lukewarm water
  5–5½ cups all-purpose flour (approximately)
     1½ cups raisins
       1 egg mixed with 2 tablespoons milk

Mix together warm milk, butter and salt. Add sugar, eggs and mashed potatoes. Dissolve the yeast in ¼ cup lukewarm water and let stand 5 minutes until bubbly. Add yeast to liquid mixture and slowly beat in 4 cups of the flour. Mix thoroughly. Stir in raisins. Turn dough out onto a floured board. Knead in 1 cup of flour, or enough more to form a fairly firm dough. Keep kneading until dough is smooth and elastic, approximately 5–10 minutes. When bubbles appear in the dough and it feels firm and holds its shape, place in buttered bowl and cover with damp towel. Let dough rise until doubled in bulk. Punch down. Knead again for a few minutes, return to bowl, cover and let rise one more time. Punch down again and let rest a few minutes. Grease two 5 x 9-inch loaf pans. Divide dough in half, shape into loaves and place in pans. Let rise until doubled. Preheat oven to 350°. Brush tops of loaves with egg-milk mixture. Bake 30–40 minutes. Test for doneness by removing from pans and thumping bottoms of loaves with fingers. If they sound hollow, bread is ready. Remove from pans and let cool on rack before eating.

Makes 2 loaves.

DR. ISADORE ROSENFELD

I T'S hard to estimate the number of hysterical parents whom pediatrician **Dr. Loraine Stern** has managed to calm down with her frequent visits to *Hour Magazine*. You can tell by her no-nonsense approach that Dr. Stern *knows* what she's talking about. She has the ability to make parents of young children feel safe and in good hands—a comforting quality that we hope all our pediatricians possess. When I asked her for a recipe, she told me she loved to cook and sent me one of her favorite appetizers. She said she serves it with cocktail rye or small slices of toasted bread.

Onion Panade

A *mellow variation of the Provençal dish. Traditionally served with bread.*

>   6 tablespoons olive oil
>   6 medium-large onions (about 2 pounds), thinly sliced
>   ½ teaspoon salt
>   1 tablespoon anise liqueur
>   1 tablespoon chopped fresh sage, *or* 1 teaspoon dried sage, crumbled
>   Niçoise olives

Heat olive oil in large, heavy skillet over low heat. Add onion, sprinkle with salt and stir to coat with oil. Cover and cook 40 minutes, stirring occasionally. Remove cover and continue cooking just until onion begins to color, about 20 minutes. Add liqueur and sage, and cook 10 more minutes. Cool to room temperature.

Spoon onion mixture into center of large platter. Garnish with olives and serve with toast or cocktail rye.

Serves 6.

DR. LORAINE STERN

Indian Barbecued Chicken

Chicken must marinate overnight. Goes well with brown rice or pita bread and a salad of onion, tomatoes and radishes.

1 3-pound chicken, skinned
  Juice of 1 lemon
1 teaspoon salt
1 teaspoon saffron (optional)
2 teaspoons coriander seeds
1 teaspoon cumin seeds
1 1-inch piece fresh ginger, chopped
2 cloves garlic, chopped
1 small onion, chopped
½ teaspoon ground red pepper
1 cup plain yogurt

Make small slashes in chicken with sharp knife. Mix lemon juice and salt, and rub into the cuts. If using saffron, cover it with 2 tablespoons boiling water and let steep for a few minutes, then pour over the chicken and let marinate for 30 minutes. Toast coriander and cumin seeds, then grind in blender with ginger, garlic, onion, red pepper and yogurt. Smear over chicken and let marinate overnight.

Next day, preheat oven to 350° and bake chicken for 1 hour, or cook on outside grill until done.

Serves 4.

JOE GRAEDON

" FIGHT Back!" Eggplant is **David Horowitz**'s recipe. America's favorite consumer expert certainly fights back the way nobody else can. But you know what I learned about him in the process of putting together this cookbook? David loves to cook and takes pride in his cooking. And I'll bet we're talking about the smartest shopper around. I always have so much fun when he's on *Hour* because he's serious and committed to helping us speak up and fight back to get what we deserve. Try his eggplant and, if you don't like it, fight back!
Write to:
David Horowitz
"Fight Back!" Eggplant
Burbank, CA 91523

"Fight Back!" Eggplant
A.K.A. Eggplant à la David

2 tablespoons olive oil
1 medium onion, sliced in thin rings
1 medium zucchini, thinly sliced on diagonal
1 medium eggplant
½ large, ripe tomato, seeded and chopped
1 clove garlic, minced
½ teaspoon dried basil
¾ cup crumbled feta cheese

Heat oil in large skillet. Add onion and sauté until golden. Add zucchini, cover, cook over medium heat for 5 minutes. Slice eggplant, cut rounds into strips 1 inch wide, add to boiling water in large saucepan, simmer 8 minutes, or until tender. Add tomato, garlic and basil to zucchini. Top with drained eggplant and feta. Heat through. Serve.

Serves 4.

DAVID HOROWITZ

I F you take away the hat, the ponytail, the Armani fashions and the French accent, you're left with a sensitive, caring soul and a brilliant talent. Of course, why would anyone want to take away the parts that make José—José? When we first introduced him on the show, there were some raised eyebrows, but before long people were fighting to line up and become one of the master's make-overs. As you might expect from a man who was born in Nice, France, José's recipe is for Salade Niçoise.

Salade Niçoise

This is José's mother's authentic recipe. He tells me that in Nice you eat this every day. José adds options for an American version—tuna fish and sliced potatoes. And he reminds you, "Shake your dressing, darling!"

1 head butter lettuce, torn up
3 tomatoes, sliced
1 cucumber, thinly sliced
1 can of anchovies
3 hard-boiled eggs, sliced
1 onion, sliced
1 small jar/can of black olives

Dressing

3 tablespoons olive oil
Juice of 1 lemon
Salt
Pepper
3 tablespoons Dijon mustard

To serve, either lightly toss salad ingredients together with dressing or, on individual plates, arrange all other ingredients on top of lettuce and sprinkle with dressing.

Serves 3–6.

JOSÉ EBER

DR. William Rader is our contributing psychiatrist. He has been on television for years, offering hope and help to millions of viewers. As he says, he may not always have the answers, but he encourages people to be able to look at the questions, confront the problems and be willing to talk about them. He thinks that's crucial. As he has said many times, he can reach more people with one appearance on *Hour Magazine* than he could in a lifetime of treating people in his office. We're glad he's a part of *Hour*. And now for his Greek Salad . . .

Greek Salad

        1 crisp head lettuce
           Olive oil
           Vinegar
           Salt and pepper
        1 medium cucumber
        3 cups whole cherry tomatoes
     1½ pounds feta cheese
           Oregano
        1 medium avocado
      ¾ pound black Greek olives

Line a platter with outer leaves of the lettuce. Tear remaining leaves into small pieces and season with a little olive oil, lots of vinegar and some salt and pepper. Arrange torn-up lettuce in a mound in center of platter. Slice the cucumber. Season with a little olive oil and lots of vinegar and some salt and pepper. Within the edge of the platter, make a ring of overlapping cucumber slices and some cherry tomato halves. Break the feta cheese into pieces and sprinkle olive oil and oregano over it. Inside the ring of cucumbers form a ring of the feta cheese pieces. Next form a ring of sliced avocado. Slice remaining cherry tomatoes in half. Pile the tomatoes mixed with the black olives and the remaining feta cheese in the center. Sprinkle the entire salad with a little olive oil, vinegar and a little bit of oregano.

Choose your preferred combination of ingredients for your own individual salad (Greek style).

Serves 6.

DR. WILLIAM RADER

DR. David Sobel is the Director of Patient Education and Health Promotion for Kaiser Permanente in Northern California. His focus is on preventive medicine, and he's helped us to understand how to use some of the new and exciting home kits that aid in early diagnosis of serious health problems. He describes himself as a doctor who firmly believes that the physician and the patient should be partners in health care, and I like that concept. His ℞ for Jelled Sauternes is unusual; while the long-term effects have not been determined, the short-term effects are delicious!

Jelled Sauternes

Sauternes is a sweet, luscious French dessert wine (not to be confused with the dry table wine, sauterne). This wine, ranging in color from a light yellow to a deep golden or amber, can be drunk along with dessert—or can become a delicious and elegant dessert in itself.

     1 bottle of French Sauternes (an inexpensive one will do just fine)
  1½ envelopes unflavored gelatin
   ½ cup granulated sugar
      Fruit or whipped cream (optional)

Begin by mixing the gelatin in ¼ cup of Sauternes. Set aside. In a separate saucepan, add the sugar to 1½ cups of Sauternes. Heat over medium heat to dissolve the sugar and bring the Sauternes just to boiling. Remove from heat, add the gelatin-Sauternes mixture and stir. Then stir in the remaining Sauternes. Pour into lightly oiled wine glasses or custard cups and chill until set, at least 6 hours. Serve chilled with raspberries, strawberries or a dab of whipped cream on top, if desired.

Serves 6–8.

DR. DAVID SOBEL

"**H**ELOISE"—for years her name has been synonymous with household hints. When we first introduced her to our audience, we surprised them. They assumed she must be much older, since the famous column was started by her mother in 1959. When her mom died, the present Heloise took over. And believe me, nobody has more suggestions or tips for combating everyday household problems than Heloise. One of the most popular hints about food that she offered was this one:

Want a good way to store onions and garlic? Take a clean pair of pantyhose, drop an onion in one foot and a garlic bulb in the other foot, then tie a knot, then drop another onion, another garlic bulb, tie a knot, etc. Keep dry and store in a place that's cool and dark (like a cellar or garage). Then, when you need onions or garlic, take your scissors and cut off whatever you need.

Don't doubt Heloise. She's a woman whose hints have been tested and tested and tested—just like her mother's wonderful recipe for Angel Biscuits, which follows.

Angel Biscuits

Great for breakfast, lunch or supper. Your family will love you for making these! You can mix these biscuits up one day and cook them the next. The dough will keep up to 3 days in a covered bowl in the refrigerator.

> 1 package dry yeast
> ¼ cup warm water
> 2½ cups all-purpose flour
> ½ teaspoon baking soda
> 1 teaspoon baking powder
> 1 teaspoon salt
> ⅛ cup granulated sugar
> ½ cup shortening
> 1 cup buttermilk

Dissolve the yeast in the warm water; set aside. Mix the dry ingredients in the order given, cutting in the shortening as you normally do for biscuits or pie dough. Stir in the buttermilk and the yeast mixture. Blend thoroughly and the dough is ready to refrigerate or roll out.

When you are ready to make these delicious biscuits, preheat oven to 400°. Turn the dough out onto a floured board and knead lightly as for regular biscuits. Roll out and cut with a biscuit cutter, placing rounds in a greased pan. Let the biscuits rise slightly before baking for about 12–15 minutes, or until lightly browned and done. If the dough is cold, it will take a little longer to rise.

Makes 8–20 biscuits.

HELOISE

ALEXANDRA Penney is the author of *How to Make Love to a Man* and *Great Sex,* two of the most successful books on the subject. While sex is often a difficult subject to talk about, Alexandra presents it in a way that doesn't offend anyone. In the past she's shared her love tips with us. She's said that one great way to start a romantic evening is with a great meal—here she's given us one good way to end a great meal too!

Instant Romantic-Exotic Dessert

    1 pint vanilla ice cream (Häagen-Dazs works best)
    ¾ cup sweetened pureed chestnuts
    ¼ cup sherry (either sweet or dry)
       Whipped cream
       Shaved chocolate

Let ice cream soften, swirl in chestnut puree and sherry. Repack ice cream in container and place in freezer. Should be served semisoft with hunks of whipped cream and shaved chocolate on top.

Serves 2–4.

ALEXANDRA PENNEY

I'VE been reading excerpts from **Dear Abby**'s book to our studio audience before the show for the past three years. It has provided me with more audience-pleasing material than any comedian could. You've all read what Abby's written for years, but I'm glad we can give you the opportunity to hear and see her; her exuberance and sense of humor combined with her sound advice reinforces your belief in her.

Since she's shared so much practical advice with our viewers, we knew she'd have a recipe to share too. Apparently about twenty-five years ago, she begged this recipe from the pastry chef at the Phoenix Hotel (in Lexington, Kentucky), which is no longer in existence, and has shared it with her readers through the years. She's received hundreds of letters raving about it, and it is her own personal favorite dessert recipe.

Abby's Pecan Pie

You can top it with a bit of whipped cream or ice cream, but even plain, nothing tops this pecan pie!

> 1 cup white corn syrup
> 1 cup dark brown sugar, firmly packed
> 1/3 teaspoon salt
> 1/3 cup melted butter
> 1 teaspoon vanilla
> 3 whole eggs, slightly beaten
> 1 9-inch unbaked pie shell
> 1 heaping cup whole pecans

Preheat oven to 350°. Mix syrup, sugar, salt, butter and vanilla. Add eggs. Mix. Pour into unbaked pie shell. Sprinkle pecans over the filling. Bake pie for approximately 45 minutes.

Confidential to Abby's Pecan Pie Bakers

The recipe states that the pie should be baked for 45–50 minutes in a preheated 350° *gas* oven. *Please note:* If an electric oven is used, add 15–20 minutes to the baking time. If a toothpick inserted in the center of the pie comes out clean, the pie is done. (Test after 45 minutes.)

Serves 6.

DEAR ABBY (ABIGAIL VAN BUREN)

MARTY Leshner, our regular travel expert, is truly one of a kind. Few people know that Marty started in this business as talent coordinator for *The Jack Paar Show* and then worked for Dinah Shore for years too. Some people never get the chance to go on a trip, but Marty's story-telling expertise gives you the feeling that you've *been there* and makes his experience a vicarious pleasure for us all.

Would you believe that a man who's traveled all over the world (to sixty countries) looks forward to coming home to one of the simplest of dishes—a Banana Split!

Marty's Banana Split

Marty tells me, "This is my favorite recipe, the enjoyment of it made infinitely better by a chance to eat it without *anyone* telling me how many calories are in it!"

First put butterscotch in the bottom of the bowl. On top, put 3 scoops of ice cream. My favorite choices:

butter pecan
jamoca almond fudge
coffee

Cut a banana in half lengthwise and put a piece on each side of ice cream. Pour a generous ladleful of hot fudge over ice cream. Sprinkle with crushed walnuts. Top with real whipped cream.

If counting calories, you do *not* need to add maraschino cherries.

Serves 1.

MARTY LESHNER

6

HOUR FAMILY IN THE KITCHEN

At last . . . the final chapter in a cookbook that I hope you'll grow fond of. For _Hour's_ "family" in the kitchen, I decided to include one of my favorite recipes. I also thought that those of you who are fans of the show would enjoy learning a little about the people who make _Hour Magazine_ happen. Naturally, the "family" members who are included head a large staff (each member of which had his or her own recipe to include, mind you), but we chose just a few staff members—those who are probably most responsible for keeping _Hour Magazine_ cooking!

DOING the cooking segments on *Hour Magazine* has given me an appreciation for cooking and a new pleasure in experimenting with recipes. It's very exciting to learn things on the show and to be able to go home and try them out. I can now prepare a recipe with a sense of confidence. But for me, one reason that the cooking segments are so enjoyable is not the obvious one: Instead it's the fact that they usually come at the end of the taping, and I am *so* relieved that the hard work and serious segments are done and I can really just be myself and relax!

Here's one of my all-time favorite recipes.

Chinese Walnut Chicken

1 teaspoon cornstarch
1 tablespoon water
1 egg white
2 large whole chicken breasts, skinned, boned and cut into 1-inch cubes
3 tablespoons soy sauce
1 tablespoon bourbon
½ teaspoon granulated sugar
4 tablespoons oil
3 green onions, cut into 2-inch slivers, both white and green parts
2 slices fresh ginger root, minced
1 clove garlic, minced
¼ cup chopped walnuts
Hot cooked rice

Mix together cornstarch, water and egg white. Add chicken and toss until thoroughly coated. Set aside. In a small bowl, combine soy sauce, bourbon and sugar. Heat skillet or wok and add 2 tablespoons of oil. Stir fry chicken for about 3–5 minutes, or until completely cooked. Remove from pan. Add remaining oil to pan and stir fry onion, ginger and garlic, 1 minute. Add soy sauce–bourbon mixture and cook quickly until sauce has thickened. Stir in walnuts. Combine with chicken. Serve with rice.

Serves 4.

GARY COLLINS

Broiled Whitefish

At one point in my life . . . cooking was a passion. It was nothing to sit in a kitchen for hours . . . poring over cookbooks . . . then going on to create an exotic meal. Some days, when I wasn't working, I would experiment with different foods for five or six hours at a time. I never got bored and was always amazed to see what could be created from raw ingredients. While I even taught cooking for a while, I always had a difficult time trying to put recipes down on paper. So much of what I did was experimental—a little of this, and a lot of that. Today, my interest is in cooking fast, healthful dishes. Gone forever the butter, the cream and thick white sauces. Actually, my recipes are rather boring for a gourmet palate, but I like keeping things simple.

2 tablespoons Dijon mustard
3 tablespoons fresh lemon juice
1 clove garlic, minced
6 tablespoons olive oil
Salt and pepper to taste
2 pieces of French bread, without crusts
2 fish filets, any type suitable for broiling

Preheat broiler. Mix together all of the above ingredients, except the French bread and the fish filets, to make the sauce. Put the French bread into the blender and make crumbs. Lay the fish on oiled pan. Drizzle half of the sauce over the fish and top with bread crumbs. Drizzle remaining sauce over bread crumbs. Broil approximately 10 minutes.

Garnish with a watercress bouquet and fresh lemon halves, if desired. Makes enough sauce for 2 large filets.

BONNIE STRAUSS

THOSE of you who have been faithful fans of the show will remember **Pat Mitchell,** my co-host for the first three years. She left *Hour* to host her own show, *Woman to Woman*, which won an Emmy for the best daytime show. Recently it has been reborn as a regular segment on NBC's *Today* show. When I asked Pat to contribute a recipe to our collection, she said she wanted to share a recipe that's been in her Southern family for years.

Her mother baked Red Velvet Cake for the family on *all* special occasions—birthdays, Fourth of July, actually, for *any* holiday. But Pat quickly added that, although she's accepted the tradition, now that she worries about calories, she bakes this cake *only* at Christmas. And to me that sounds like a perfect time to enjoy this festive dessert. So why not splurge?

Red Velvet Cake

1½ cups granulated sugar
1½ cups Wesson oil
2 eggs
2 tablespoons cocoa powder
2 ounces red food coloring
1 tablespoon vinegar
1 teaspoon salt
1 teaspoon baking soda
2½ cups all-purpose flour
1 cup buttermilk

Filling

1 8-ounce package cream cheese
1 stick (½ cup) butter or margarine
1 box confectioners' sugar
1 teaspoon vanilla
1 cup pecans or other nuts (optional)

Preheat oven to 350°. Mix granulated sugar and oil together. Add eggs, cocoa, food coloring and vinegar. Sift together the salt, soda and flour. Add to the sugar-and-oil mixture, alternating with the buttermilk. Mix well. Bake in 3 greased and floured small, round cake pans for 30 minutes. Remove from pans and let cool on racks.

To prepare filling, cream together cream cheese, butter, confectioners' sugar and vanilla. Stir in nuts, if desired. After cake cools, spread filling on each layer and assemble cake.

Note

Put filling between layers and on top, but not on sides—so you can see the red on the sides of the cake

PAT MITCHELL

H OUR *Magazine*'s director, **Glen Swanson,** is one of the most dependable in television. But besides being an award-winning director, he's probably the most personable and pleasant member of the staff, *even* when he's under pressure. Glen directed the *Dinah Shore* show for years, and it's no wonder that he never misses an ingredient or a shot during our cooking segments. He gave us one of his favorite recipes for Veal Scallopini.

Veal Scallopini

Can also be made with chicken breast to help hold down the cost. Serve with noodles or rice, green salad and a vegetable.

> 4 ⅜-inch-thick veal cutlets (about 4 ounces each)
> ½ pound fresh mushrooms, thinly sliced
> ¼ cup butter
> 2 tablespoons olive oil
> 1 small onion, finely chopped
> ¼ cup dry sherry
> 2 teaspoons all-purpose flour
> ½ cup beef broth
> ¼ teaspoon salt
> ⅛ teaspoon pepper
> 2 tablespoons heavy cream

Pound veal cutlets until ¼ inch thick, or less. Pat dry with paper towels. In a 12-inch skillet over medium heat, sauté mushrooms in butter until light brown, 3–4 minutes. With slotted spoon, remove mushrooms to bowl; reserve. Add oil to butter remaining in skillet, heat over medium heat. Add veal, sauté, turning once, until light brown, 2–3 minutes per side. Remove veal to plate; reserve. Add onion to skillet, sauté until tender, 2–3 minutes. Stir sherry into onion in skillet. Heat to boiling over medium-high heat; boil 15 seconds. Stir in flour. Cook, stirring constantly, 30 seconds. Remove from heat; stir in broth. Cook uncovered over medium heat, stirring constantly, to boiling. Stir reserved mushrooms and the salt and pepper into sauce. Add reserved veal; reduce heat to low. Simmer covered until veal is tender, about 8 minutes. Remove from heat. Push veal to one side of skillet. Stir cream into sauce, mixing well. Heat over low heat just until heated thoroughly. Serve immediately.

Serves 4.

GLEN SWANSON

TGIM. Thank God It's Monday is the motto of the show's producer, **Steve Clements.** Nobody works harder than Steve or is more committed to the show. He's a workaholic and he cooks up the staff to a feverish pitch, but his amazing sense of humor wins everyone over to his side, no matter how hard he drives them. How he has time to eat dinner, let alone cook it, is really beyond me. As you can see, he asked his mother to send us her Mandelbrodt recipe. Steve also offered his soon-to-be-famous recipe for barbecued steak. Sounds *just* like him!

Minna's Mandelbrodt

3 cups sifted all-purpose flour
1 tablespoon baking powder
  Pinch of salt
4 eggs
1 cup granulated sugar
¾ cup vegetable oil
1 teaspoon vanilla
1 teaspoon lemon flavoring, *or* 1 teaspoon grated lemon rind
1 cup chopped walnuts
½ cup mini chocolate chips
½ cup raisins (optional)
2 tablespoons granulated sugar
1 tablespoon cinnamon

Preheat oven to 350°. Sift together flour, baking powder and salt. Set aside. Beat together eggs and 1 cup sugar until creamy. Add the oil, vanilla and lemon flavoring, and mix well. Gradually add flour mixture. Stir in nuts, chocolate chips and raisins, if desired. Mix well.

Shape into 3 loaves on a slightly greased baking sheet. Sprinkle with a mixture of 2 tablespoons sugar and 1 tablespoon cinnamon. Bake for 30 minutes. Cool and cut into ½-inch slices.

Makes about 30–40 cookies.

STEVE CLEMENTS

Steve's Special Barbecued Steak

Buy 2 too large T-bone steaks, too much for one meal, and not enough for a second.

Trim the fat with a dull knife, so that it takes twice as long. Take broad strokes, so that enough meat is removed with the fat, enabling the dog to be fed without your feeling too much guilt.

Place steaks in a shallow dish. Add enough soy sauce so that it reaches the rim of the plate. This ensures "spillage" on the Dhurrie rug on your way to the outdoor barbecue.

How to Barbecue: Turn the gas on high. While the gas escapes, feverishly remove two extra-long matches from the box. Light one and allow wind to blow it out. Quickly light the grill; make sure you're close enough so that when ignition takes place, you're blown back and your hair is just singed.

Pace impatiently, and put the steak on before the grill is hot enough, allowing juices to seep out while the steak cooks.

Speak casually with your wife, and forget how much time has gone by since you put the steaks on.

When your wife asks if the steak is ready to be turned over, say "Almost." Casually stride out and flip the steaks. Don't forget to pour the soy sauce remaining in the dish over the steaks. This guarantees an exciting flame show, causing charring.

With long tongs, quickly remove the now well-done steaks from the barbecue.

Carry the steaks back over the Dhurrie rug—don't worry! When you turned the plate of soy sauce over the steak, enough traveled to the underside of the plate to provide those extra couple of spots on the rug.

Then set the table, pour the wine and have the salad, leaving enough time for the steak to cool. *Bon Appétit!*

Serves 2 too much.

STEVE CLEMENTS

MARTY Berman, our executive producer, is an Emmy-winning producer with a sterling reputation in the industry, even though he's still quite young. When I think back over the years of working with him I've got to say that his support and belief in me are what have been most important. His extraordinary judgment and creativity are what have made our show one of the most successful in the history of daytime television. Marty somehow manages always to seem calm and nonchalant while he pulls all the strings necessary to keep the staff content and happy and the show running smoothly.

Marty, who has never forgotten his roots and the warm memories of his mother's kitchen, decided to make his all-time favorite recipe backstage one day. A few hours after it started cooking, people from all over the lot came around wanting to know what the marvelous smell was.

Cholent

Cholent goes back as far as the days of the Second Temple, some thousands of years ago. For Orthodox Jews, cooking is not permitted on the Sabbath, so long before the slow-cooker was developed, the women came up with a great idea: They could avoid cooking on Saturday if they made the meal on Friday and cooked it very slowly overnight over the lowest possible flame. That's probably how this recipe started. It's traditionally served for the big meal (lunchtime) on the Sabbath.

   5 pounds potatoes
   1 package lima beans (optional)
   1 package barley (optional)
   1 large piece of brisket (5–7 pounds) or short ribs (optional)
   1 16-ounce jar of honey
   1 whole onion

   Peel and cut potatoes into quarters. Put in a 10-quart stockpot and fill to the top with salted water. Add lima beans, barley and brisket, if desired. Add the onion (whole) for flavor. Pour half the jar of honey over the top and place pot, covered, over a very low flame. After about 6 hours, add remainder of honey. Potatoes will start turning golden.

   The most important part of the recipe . . . leave it alone and wait for the smell to attack you in the middle of the night while you're sleeping. It's at this point that you should be prepared to open the doors to all your neighbors, who will want to know what that wonderful smell is!

Total amount of cooking time is approximately 18 hours, or until potatoes have turned a rich brown.

Suggestion: Try the basics first and then experiment with adding the options.

Serves 12–16.

MARTIN BERMAN

IF there was an MVP award for the cooking segments, this next gentleman would win it hands down! **Chris Circosta** is one of the real unsung heroes on the show. I've already dedicated this book to Chris, because there's no question that none of the cooking segments could ever have been achieved without our indispensable prop master. He buys the ingredients, cooks them, makes them look good and makes sure the cooking segments run smoothly. So the next time you're sitting at home watching the show and you see me take the finished product out of our magic oven, know that the magic is Chris!

Stracciatella with Chicken Meatballs

Chicken Meatballs

 ½ pound ground chicken
 ¼ cup Italian bread crumbs
 1 egg
 1 teaspoon minced garlic
 2 tablespoons minced parsley
 2 tablespoons grated Parmesan cheese
   Salt and pepper
 2 tablespoons butter

Soup

 6 cups chicken broth
 ¼ teaspoon salt
 ⅛ teaspoon white pepper
 ⅛ pound angel's hair, coil fideo or vermicelli noodles,
     uncooked
   Chicken Meatballs (see above)

½ cup chopped spinach
3 eggs
¼ cup grated Parmesan or Romano cheese
Grated lemon peel, for garnish
Chopped parsley, for garnish

To prepare meatballs, combine all ingredients, except butter, in a mixing bowl. Mix thoroughly. Form into small meatballs, approximately 24 total. Melt butter in medium-size skillet. Brown meatballs in butter. Drain on paper towels.

Heat broth to a boil, season with salt and pepper. Add noodles and Chicken Meatballs. Reduce heat and simmer for 20 minutes. Add spinach. Cook for additional 5 minutes. Raise heat; when soup is almost at a boil, stir in eggs gradually, add cheese. Serve immediately. Garnish with lemon peel and parsley.

Serves 4–6.

CHRIS CIRCOSTA

INDEX